Target Spelling
& Vocabulary Skills

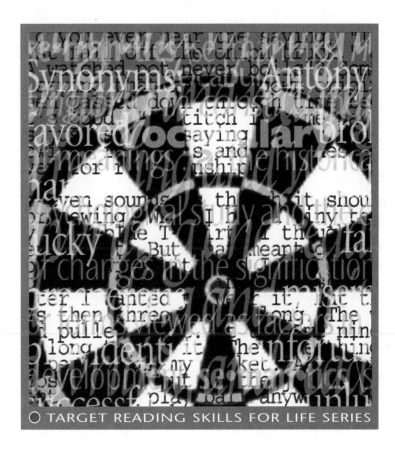

○ TARGET READING SKILLS FOR LIFE SERIES

AGS
PUBLISHING

Circle Pines, Minnesota 55014-1796
800-328-2560
www.agsnet.com

Cover Design
Sarah Bennett

Photo and Illustration Credits
Page 6, © Tom Stewart/CORBIS; p. 19, © Richard Price/FPG International; p. 21 (all), Judy King Rieniets; p. 34, © 1996 CORBIS/original image courtesy NASA/CORBIS; p. 41 (all), Roberta Collier-Morales/Portfolio Solutions; p. 63, © Charles Gupton/CORBISSTOCKMARKET.COM; p. 83, © Craig Aurness/CORBIS; p. 89, © Reg Charity/CORBIS; p. 101 (all), Judy King Rieniets; p. 109, Joel Snyder/Portfolio Solutions

Publisher's Project Staff
Associate Director, Product Development: Teri Mathews; Assistant Editor: Haley Lasché; Development Assistant: Bev Johnson; Design Manager: Nancy Condon; Senior Designer: Daren Hastings; Technical Specialist: Laura Henrichsen; Purchasing Agent: Mary Kaye Kuzma; Marketing Manager/Curriculum: Brian Holl

Development and editorial services by Straight Line Editorial Development, Inc.
Art direction by Sally Brewer Lawrence

Product Number 93714
ISBN 0-7854-3371-6

A 0 9 8 7 6 5 4 3 2 1

CONTENTS

CONTENTS

INTRODUCTION

Welcome!

Words are all around us. We use them when we think, speak, listen, and write. This book will help you use words more effectively when you write.

Here are some of the things you'll learn:

■ **Use simple letter patterns to help you spell words.** Many words follow the same pattern of letters. Knowing the patterns can help you spell many words—even words you think you don't know how to spell.

■ **Learn spelling strategies.** Some spelling patterns are hard to predict. This book will show you how spelling strategies can help.

■ **Understand letters and sounds.** Knowing how letters and sounds work together helps you to spell words right.

■ **Build word power.** The more words you know, the more word power you have. This book will teach you many words that are useful in school and in daily life.

■ **Understand how words change.** Words can change, depending on how they're used. This book will show you how words change, and what the changes mean.

With practice and a little help from this book, you'll be a word pro in no time.

SPELLING TIPS

These tips will help you to spell words correctly when you write:

- ◼ **Listen to the sounds.** Listen for the sounds you hear at the beginning, in the middle, and at the end of a word.

- ◼ **Think about letters.** Ask yourself: **What letters or letter patterns usually stand for the sounds in this word?**

- ◼ **Think about meaning.** Should you write **hair** or **hare**? Is the word you want spelled **won** or **one**? **Sun** or **son**? Thinking about how the word is used in a sentence will help you know which spelling to use.

- ◼ **Picture the word.** Make a mental picture of the word. Think about its shape and length.

- ◼ **Check the word.** Look at the word after you've written it. Does it look right? If you're not sure, check it in a dictionary.

WORD STUDY TIPS

The Five Steps to Learning a Word

1. **Read the word.** Notice its shape. Is it long or short? What letters does it begin with? Does it look like other words you know?

2. **Say the word.** What sounds does it have? Which letters stand for those sounds?

3. **Write the word.** Get a feel for the word by writing it down.

4. **Practice reading the word.** Read the word again and again until you know it.

5. **Use the word.** Add the word to your vocabulary, both when speaking and writing.

CHAPTER 1

LESSON 1   Short Vowels/CVC

KNOW

■ The words **tap, net, lip, hop,** and **nut** all have a short vowel sound.

■ These words have the Consonant-Vowel-Consonant, or CVC, pattern.

Word Bank

Read each word in the Word Bank. Then read the sentence beside it.

cap	A **cap** with a bill will keep the sun off.
pick	The kids **pick** beets by hand.
rot	Wet sticks will **rot**.
beg	My dogs **beg** for treats.
rug	Tim got mud on the **rug**.
drop	Do not **drop** those eggs!
shun	Those kids are mean, so we will **shun** them.
pest	That cat can be a **pest**!
flip	Can you **flip** the chops on the grill?
slam	Did you see that truck **slam** into the pole?

Sort: Write each word from the Word Bank under the vowel sound it has.

short **a**	short **e**	short **i**	short **o**	short **u**
1._____	3._____	5._____	7._____	9._____
2._____	4._____	6._____	8._____	10._____

Complete: Write a vowel in each blank to spell a word that fits the sentence.

11. That meat will r___t if you keep it in the sun.

12. If you stand up, the raft will fl___p!

13. If you have the red c___p on, I will see you.

14. This r___g feels soft.

15. Nick will b___g for a bite of your cake.

Match: Draw a line from each word to its meaning.

16. rot   • to turn over

17. beg   • to shut hard

18. shun   • to go bad

19. pest   • to keep away from

20. flip   • to ask for

21. slam   • kid or animal that bugs you

SPELLING BUILDER

Some words have the CVC pattern but do not have the usual short vowel sound. **Won** and **few** are two of these words.

Choose: Write a word from the box to complete each sentence.

rug	pick	cap	drop

22. That pine will _____ its cones on the grass.

23. We need a new _____ in the den.

24. I want to _____ a name for the pup.

25. Nick put on his _____.

Proofread: Read each sentence. Draw a line through the misspelled word. Write the correct spelling on the line.

26. His pups bayg for scraps. _____

27. Ken will slamm the next pitch over the creek. _____

28. My cat can be a peste. _____

29. Nali will filp the rug when she sweeps. _____

30. Sam has a kap with a red bill. _____

31. The kids down the street pik plums for jam. _____

Write: Write a sentence to answer each question.

32. What is one thing a kid must not drop?

_____

33. If you could pick a new cap, what kind would you pick?

_____

LESSON 2   Long Vowels/CVC*e* and Long *e*

KNOW

■ If there are two vowels in a word and one is final **e**, the first vowel usually stands for a long sound. The final **e** is silent. This is called the CVCe pattern.

■ The long **e** sound is often spelled **ee** or **ea**.

Word Bank

Read each word in the Word Bank. Then read the sentence beside it.

vine	There must be 50 grapes on that **vine**.
flame	Keep your hand out of the **flame**.
hope	I **hope** Nina picks me for the team.
lean	Willa likes to eat **lean** beef.
tube	You can have fun with this **tube** in the lake.
meek	Jack seems **meek**, but he is brave.
rude	It is **rude** to yell in class.
glide	The ducks **glide** on the pond.
slope	Can you hike up this **slope**?
crave	My pals **crave** sweets, but I like nuts.

Sort: Write each word from the Word Bank under the vowel sound it has.

long **a**	long **e**	long **i**	long **o**	long **u**
1._____	3._____	5._____	7._____	9._____
2._____	4._____	6._____	8._____	10._____

Complete: Write a vowel and a silent e in the blanks to spell a word that fits the sentence.

11. Step on this pump and fill up the t___b___.

12. Sue's home is at the top of a steep sl___p___.

13. Nate will trim the v___n___ on the gate.

14. A draft made the fl___m___ go out.

15. Did you see that r___d___ man cut in line?

Solve: Use words from the Word Bank to fill in the puzzle.

Across
18. comes from a match
20. has a long stem
21. shy

Down
16. has a tilt
17. has no fat
19. to move in a smooth way

Choose: Write a word from the box to complete each sentence.

hope	rude	tube	crave

22. Is it _____ to grab a pen from a kid's hand?

23. I _____ a treat, but no one has one for me.

24. My pals _____ the sun shines next week.

25. You must not take that _____ down the slide.

Proofread: Read each sentence. Draw a line through the misspelled word. Write the correct spelling on the line.

26. It is not safe to skate down that sloap. _____

27. Did you see the sled glid down the slope? _____

28. Help me pick beans off this vin. _____

29. That flaim can set off a blaze. _____

30. I like to swim with a toob. _____

31. Stella is meak, and Casey is rude. _____

Write: Write a sentence to answer each question.

32. How many pals would come to help you with a big job?

_____

33. What class do you have next?

_____

LESSON 3   Plurals

KNOW

■ Making a word tell about more than one is called making it **plural**.

■ Add **es** instead of **s** to words that end in **x, z, ch, sh,** or **s** to make them plural.

Word Bank

Read each word in the Word Bank. Then read the sentence beside it.

scales	Most fish have **scales**.
boxes	Pat stacked the **boxes** by my desk.
dens	Foxes keep their pups in their **dens**.
buses	On Friday the **buses** were all late.
skills	If you have **skills**, you can get a job.
passes	The kids on the team had **passes** to skip class.
speeches	Dave gives **speeches** and asks for votes.
spots	Rita's dog has black **spots**.
wishes	You can make three **wishes**.
clumps	Rocky has **clumps** of mud on his soles.

Sort: Write each word from the Word Bank under the rule that tells about it.

Add **s** to tell about more than one

1. _____

2. _____

3. _____

4. _____

5. _____

Add **es** to tell about more than one

6. _____

7. _____

8. _____

9. _____

10. _____

Complete: Write **s** or **es** to spell each plural word.

11. wish_____

12. skill_____

13. den_____

14. bus_____

15. box_____

16. scale_____

17. pass_____

18. speech_____

19. spot_____

20. clump_____

Circle: Circle the word that means almost the same as the bold word.

21. spots	slops	slots	dots
22. boxes	crates	foxes	bones
23. passes	wishes	slips	buses
24. clumps	sinks	bunches	skills
25. dens	decks	pens	holes
26. wishes	winches	hopes	watches

SPELLING BUILDER

A few words do not add **s** or **es** to tell about more than one. For example, **child** changes to **children**, and **woman** changes to **women**.

Choose: Write a word from the box to complete each pair.

skills	buses	scales	speeches

27. trucks and _____

28. fins and _____

29. _____ and votes

30. _____ and jobs

Proofread: Read each sentence. Draw a line through the misspelled word. Write the correct spelling on the line.

31. The big green beasts in those dens have scails. _____

32. Grab those clumpes of weeds and put them in boxes. _____

33. I will give passes to the kids who will give speechs. _____

34. You need many skills to drive bus's. _____

35. The buses have spotts on their sides. _____

36. Kids like to make wishs for fun. _____

Write: Write a sentence to answer each question.

37. What are the best skills you have?

_____

38. What are some beasts that live in dens?

_____

LESSON 4   Adding *-ed* or *-ing*

KNOW

- You can add **ed** and **ing** to many verbs.

- If a verb ends with two consonants, just add **ed** or **ing**. Do not drop or add any letters.

Word Bank

Read each word in the Word Bank. Then read the sentence beside it.

missing	Our cat has been **missing** for six days.
locked	Shalana **locked** the gate.
helping	Five kids are **helping** to pack the boxes.
rented	My mom **rented** a van last week.
dumping	A man is **dumping** trash in the lot down the street.
packed	My bags are **packed**, and I am all set to go.
crashing	Big waves are **crashing** on the beach.
listed	The cost of each hat is **listed** on this page.
resting	Nick is **resting** in the shade.
passed	We just **passed** the last rest stop.

Build: Write each word from the Word Bank on the correct line.

1. rest + ing = _____
2. miss + ing = _____
3. crash + ing = _____
4. help + ing = _____
5. dump + ing = _____

6. pack + ed = _____
7. pass + ed = _____
8. rent + ed = _____
9. lock + ed = _____
10. list + ed = _____

Complete: Write **ed** or **ing** in each blank to spell a word that fits the sentence.

11. LuAnn is help_____ us with math.

12. You must keep the shed lock_____.

13. Pablo has list_____ all the codes on one page.

14. Wilda ran three laps without rest_____.

15. My dad pack_____ a lunch for us.

Solve: Write a word from the Word Bank to solve each riddle.

16. socks put in a box _____

17. not here, not there _____

18. went by on the fly _____

19. lending a hand _____

20. flat on my back but not sleeping _____

21. safe inside a safe _____

WRITING TIP

When you write, circle any words you're not sure you have spelled correctly. Then, when you're done writing, go back and check the dictionary for the spelling of each circled word.

Choose: Write a word from the box to complete each sentence.

listed	dumping	rented	crashing

22. Toby _____ a DVD that we have seen a lot.

23. Who is that man _____ trash on the street?

24. The tasks are _____ on a sheet by the gate.

25. That stack of cans may come _____ down!

Proofread: Read each sentence. Draw a line through the misspelled word. Write the correct spelling on the line.

26. My mother rentd a van for the trip. _____

27. A big van just pased our truck. _____

28. The dogs are restig by the trees. _____

29. Have you seen the mising note pad? _____

30. No one loked the gate. _____

31. The names of your pals are lisded on the last page. _____

Write: Write a sentence to answer each question.

32. What is one thing you are missing?

_____

33. What were some things you packed for your last trip?

_____

LESSON 5 Adding -ed or -ing (Dropping or Doubling Letters)

KNOW

- If a word ends in a short vowel and a consonant, double the final consonant before adding **ed** or **ing**.
  Example:
  drip + ing = dripping

- If a word has a long vowel, a consonant, and a silent **e** at its end, drop the **e** before adding **ed** or **ing**.
  Example:
  shape + ing = shaping

Word Bank

Read each word in the Word Bank. Then read the sentence beside it.

scraping — The kids are **scraping** mud off their soles.
dripped — The spilled milk **dripped** onto the rug.
shaped — Jamir **shaped** the trees by clipping them.
skipping — We are **skipping** lunch, so we will need a snack.
hoping — Tim is **hoping** to catch a fish.
tapped — The chick **tapped** its beak on the glass.
choked — Sadao **choked** on the chips he was eating.
begging — Tell the dog to stop **begging** for scraps.
biting — A bug is **biting** my leg.
slipped — My bike **slipped** on the wet street.

Sort: Write each word from the Word Bank in the correct place.

double final consonant, add **ed**	double final consonant, add **ing**	drop e, add **ed**	drop e, add **ing**
1._____	4._____	6._____	8._____
2._____	5._____	7._____	9._____
3._____			10._____

Write: Write the word formed from the short word and the ending.

11. tap + ed = _____

12. bite + ing = _____

13. shape + ed = _____

14. drip + ed = _____

15. hope + ing = _____

Solve: Use words from the Word Bank to fill in the puzzle.

Across
16. sinking teeth into it
18. rubbing
20. made drops
21. asking

Down
17. hit just a bit
19. gagged

READING TIP

How do you know if a vowel is long or short? The vowel before a double consonant and **ed** or **ing** is usually short, as in **hopped**. The vowel before a single consonant and **ed** or **ing** is usually long, as in **hoped**.

Choose: Write a word from the box to complete each sentence.

slipped	shaped	skipping	hoping

22. The kids are _____ for sun.

23. Ines _____ on the tiles and fell.

24. Is Bill late, or is he _____ this class?

25. Five pals _____ the sand to make a pig.

Proofread: Read each sentence. Draw a line through the misspelled word. Write the correct spelling on the line.

26. Plum jam driped from the pot. _____

27. Zina is hopeing for a prize. _____

28. A flea is bitting your neck! _____

29. Carl shapd the meat into a patty. _____

30. I chocked on a pit at lunch. _____

31. A spy tappeed out a list in code. _____

Write: Write a sentence to answer each question.

32. What have you slipped on?

_____

33. What is one thing you are hoping for?

_____

LESSON 6 Consonant Combinations *sh, th, ch, tch*

KNOW

■ The letters **sh** usually stand for the sound at the beginning of **shape**.

■ The letters **th** usually stand for the sound at the beginning of **thin**, or at the beginning of **this**.

■ The letters **ch** usually stand for the sound at the beginning of **chop**.

■ The letters **tch** usually stand for the sound at the end of **patch**.

Word Bank

Read each word in the Word Bank. Then read the sentence beside it.

shift	Did the wind just **shift**?
throne	The king sat on the **throne** all day.
cheap	Ray sits in the **cheap** seats at games.
batch	The peaches in this **batch** are sweet.
shame	Nora will feel **shame** if she cuts in line.
thank	I must **thank** you for the gift you sent.
flash	Did you see that **flash** in the sky?
path	This **path** leads to the top of the hill.
chill	The kids felt a **chill** as the sun went down.
sketch	L.R. made a **sketch** on a big pad.

Sort: Write each word from the Word Bank in the correct place.

begins with **sh**	begins with **th**	begins with **ch**
1. _____	4. _____	7. _____
2. _____	5. _____	8. _____
ends with sh	**ends with th**	**ends with tch**
3. _____	6. _____	9. _____
		10. _____

Complete: Write sh, th, ch, or tch in each blank to spell a word that fits the sentence.

11. If it costs a dime, it is _____eap.

12. If you get a neat gift, you must say _____ank you.

13. If you get a _____ill, why not sit by a hot stove?

14. If you take a hike, keep on the pa_____.

15. If you pick bunches of grapes, you can make a ba_____ of jam.

Solve: Write a word from the Word Bank to solve each riddle.

16. I am a seat fit for a king. _____

17. I can make you blink if you see me. _____

18. I was one way, but now I am another way. _____

19. I am a feeling you have when you are rude. _____

20. You can make me with a pen and a pad. _____

21. I do not cost much. _____

22. I am not as wide as a street. _____

23. You do this when you have gotten help. _____

24. I can have five or ten, twenty or fifty. _____

25. I will make you seek the heat. _____

VOCABULARY BUILDER

Just add **y** to many words to make adjectives (describing words). For example, you can add **y** to **flash** to make **flashy** or **shift** to make **shifty**. What is a **shifty** character like?

Proofread: Read each sentence. Draw a line through the misspelled word. Write the correct spelling on the line.

26. Kenji will take a scone from this bach. _____

27. Did you see that red falsh in the sky? _____

28. Chepe locks get stuck. _____

29. The ducks will shifft their path to the west. _____

30. Marty made a scetch of our cat. _____

31. The green stones on the trone shone in the sun. _____

Write: Write a sentence to answer each question.

32. What is one good thing you have that was cheap?

_____

33. When there is a chill in the air, what do you put on?

_____

_____

Ray and Nora feel a chill.

LESSON 7   Two-Syllable Words: Names of Animals

KNOW

- A **syllable** is a word part. A word can have one or more syllables.

- Every syllable has a vowel sound. You can count the syllables in a word by listening to the number of vowel sounds.

- A first syllable that has the Consonant-Vowel-Consonant (CVC) pattern often has a short vowel sound.

- A first syllable that has the Consonant-Vowel pattern often has a long vowel sound.

Word Bank

Read each word in the Word Bank. Then read the sentence beside it.

lemur	A **lemur** spends most of its life in trees.
chipmunk	A **chipmunk** has big cheeks.
camel	A **camel** has one or two humps.
python	A **python** will give you a hug, but it will not feel good.
panda	A **panda** has a black and white coat.
puma	A **puma** is a big cat.
wombat	A **wombat** is a mammal of Australia.
raven	A **raven** can fly well.
bobcat	A **bobcat** hunts rabbits.
bison	A **bison** eats grass.

Sort: Write each word from the Word Bank in the correct place.

first syllable has a long vowel

first syllable does not have a long vowel

1._____   3._____   6._____   9._____

2._____   4._____   7._____   10._____

5._____   8._____

Complete: Write the missing first syllable to spell a word that fits the sentence.

11. A _____thon is a big snake.

12. A _____munk likes nuts.

13. A _____mur can swing from a branch.

14. A _____el can go for a long time with no drinks.

15. A _____bat has its home in the land down under.

Label: Write the animal's name under each picture. Use the Word Bank to help you.

16. _____   17. _____   18. _____

19. _____   20. _____   21. _____

Complete: Write a word from the box to complete each sentence.

camel	puma	chipmunk	bobcat

22. A _____ is a small wild cat.

23. A _____ is a bigger wild cat.

24. A _____ must hide from all wild cats!

25. A _____ has long legs.

SPELLING BUILDER

Watch out for animal names. The names of many animals have unusual spellings for vowel sounds. For example, in **monkey**, the letter **o** stands for the short **u** sound.

Proofread: Read each sentence. Draw a line through the misspelled word. Write the correct spelling on the line.

26. A panda likes to eat bamboo, but a chipmonk likes nuts. _____

27. A wombet digs, and a raven makes a nest. _____

28. A pooma is swift, and so is a bobcat. _____

29. Can a python eat a camal? _____

Write: Write a sentence to answer each question.

30. Which animal on this page gives you the creeps?

_____

31. Why is a bobcat not a good pet?

_____

LESSON 8   Names of States and Countries

KNOW

- Most states have tricky spellings. You have to learn them one by one.

- Most countries also have tricky spellings. You must study these one by one, too.

Word Bank

Read each word in the Word Bank. Then read the sentence beside it.

Texas	Texas is one of the biggest states.
China	China is one of the biggest countries.
Syria	Syria is on the Mediterranean Sea.
Montana	Montana is called the "Big Sky State."
Canada	Canada is the largest country in North America.
New York	New York is the state with the biggest city in the United States.
Ghana	Ghana is a country in West Africa.
Mexico	Mexico is next to the United States.
Kentucky	Kentucky is a state with many horses.
Ohio	Ohio is north of Kentucky.

Sort: Write each word from the Word Bank in the correct place.

States		Countries	
1._____	4._____	6._____	9._____
2._____	5._____	7._____	10._____
3._____		8._____	

Complete: Write the missing letter or letters in each name.

11. M ___ ___ ico

12. Ca ___ ___ da

13. New Y ___ ___ k

14. O ___ ___ o

15. S __ ria

16. Gha ___ ___

17. Kentu ___ ___ y

18. M ___ ntana

19. Ch ___ na

20. T ___ ___ as

Label: Write the name of the state on each blank. Use the Word Bank to help you.

21. _____

22. _____

23. _____

24. _____

25. _____

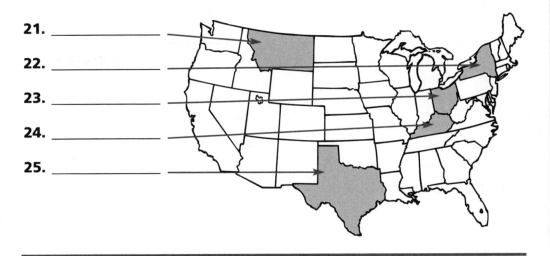

Label More: Write the name of the country on each blank. Use the Word Bank to help you.

26. _____

27. _____

28. _____

29. _____

30. _____

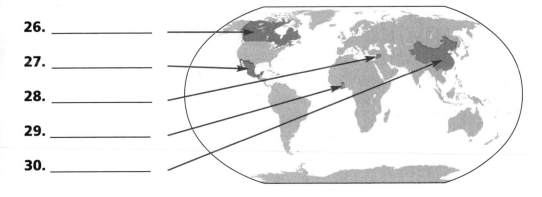

Write: Write a sentence to answer each question.

31. Which state would you like to visit? Why?

_____

_____

32. Which country would you like to visit? Why?

_____

_____

Part A

Complete: For each set, write a word from the list to complete each sentence.

drop	**A**
rug	
lean	
slope	

1. If you _____ on the glass case, it may crack.
2. You can _____ your note in the box.
3. Vicki spilled punch on the _____.
4. The kids ran up a steep _____.

speeches	**B**
skills	
passed	
resting	

5. The speedy van _____ the bus.
6. Leaders make _____ on the Fourth of July.
7. You need _____ to fix a bike.
8. Anna was sleepy, so she is _____.

hoping	**C**
slipped	
cheap	
batch	

9. Rich and Sue made a _____ of cookies.
10. We are _____ that it will be sunny for the game.
11. Sam _____ and fell on the ice.
12. I will get that hat if it is _____.

raven	**D**
panda	
New York	
Texas	

13. The state of _____ has many ranches.
14. The state of _____ has the biggest city in the United States.
15. A _____ is a black bird.
16. A _____ is a big black and white animal.

Sort: For each set, write the words in the correct place.

drop	**E**
rug	
lean	
slope	

short vowel	long vowel
17. _____	19. _____
18. _____	20. _____

speeches	**F**
passed	
resting	
skills	

adds **s**	adds **es**
21. _____	23. _____
adds **ed**	adds **ing**
22. _____	24. _____

Complete: Write the missing letter or letters to spell each word. Look at the lists on page 24 if you need help.

25. rest__ng

26. Te__as

27. ch__ __p

28. r__g

29. skill__

30. hopi__ __

31. p__nda

32. sl__p__

33. speech__ __

34. r__ven

35. l__ __n

36. N__ __ York

37. dr__p

38. ba__ch

39. slipp__ __

40. pa__ __ed

Proofread: Read each sentence. Draw a line through the misspelled word. Write the correct spelling on the line.

41. The raven has a nest in the tree on the sloap. _____

42. Nick is hopeing to see a panda. _____

43. Was that rug made in New Yorek? _____

44. Ricky passed us, and then he sliped and fell. _____

45. Please do not dropp that batch of scones. _____

46. Rhonda needs a chepe ticket to Texas. _____

47. Those who give speechs need good speaking skills. _____

48. Unless you are resting, do not leane on that pole. _____

Write: Write a sentence to answer each question.

49. When you think of Texas, what do you picture?

_____

_____

50. What is the steepest slope you know of?

_____

_____

Part B

Complete: **For each set, write a word from the list to complete each sentence.**

shun   **A**

1. A _____ man may not speak up.
2. I often _____ a snack after running.
3. The kid with the red bike is a _____!
4. Why did Larry _____ his pals last week?

pest

meek

crave

clumps   **B**

5. Foxes live in _____.
6. My best hat is _____.
7. Who tracked _____ of mud into our home?
8. My mom _____ a boat for us to use.

dens

rented

missing

scraping   **C**

9. That _____ looks just like you.
10. Dad is _____ egg off the pan.
11. Marci _____ her pen on the desk.
12. Is the queen sitting on the _____?

tapped

throne

sketch

lemur   **D**

13. A _____ puts seeds in its cheeks.
14. _____ is a country in the Middle East.
15. A _____ lives in trees.
16. _____ is a country in Africa.

chipmunk

Syria

Ghana

Match: **Draw a line from each word to its meaning.**

E

17. pest   • to make a picture fast
18. throne   • a thing that bugs others
19. sketch   • like a monkey
20. lemur   • a seat for a king or queen

F

21. rented   • rubbing hard
22. shun   • paid cash to use
23. missing   • to keep away from
24. scraping   • cannot be found

Solve: Use the words from the lists on page 26 to fill in the puzzle.

Across
25. rubbing off
29. a monkey-like animal
30. gobs or globs
32. country in Africa
34. paid for its use
36. to make a picture fast
39. cannot be found

Down
26. an animal with big cheeks
27. bothers you
28. country in the Middle East
31. to want badly
33. where a king sits
35. animal homes
37. stay away from
38. hit softly

Proofread: Read each sentence. Draw a line through the misspelled word. Write the correct spelling on the line.

40. The pest tappd on her desk all day. _____

41. A chippmunk ran to the bench and jumped up. _____

42. A lemur is a meke animal. _____

43. Are you going to Syria or Ganha on your trip? _____

44. Ben is scrapeing clumps of mud off his clogs. _____

45. I crave fun, so I reneted a jet boat. _____

46. Here is a skech of the missing man. _____

47. The queen on the thorne will shun her pals. _____

48. How many animals live in those denes? _____

Write: Write a sentence to answer each question.

49. What kind of person might you shun?

_____

50. What are some things you crave on a hot day?

_____

TEST TIP

When you finish a test, take time to look it over again. Make sure you answered every question. Try it now! Look back over this practice test. Did you complete every item?

LESSON 9   Long *i* and Long *o*

KNOW

■ Many patterns can stand for the long **i** sound besides **i-Consonant-e**.

■ The letters **y, igh, i,** and **ie** can stand for long **i**.

■ Many patterns can stand for the long **o** sound besides **o-Consonant-e**.

■ The letters **oa** and **ow** can stand for long **o**.

Word Bank

Read each word in the Word Bank. Then read the sentence beside it.

float	That stick will **float** on the lake.
slight	Noemi has a **slight** case of the flu.
tried	A crow **tried** to pick up a shiny dime.
shoal	You must keep your boat off the rocky **shoal**.
shy	Tim is **shy**, so he does not like the meetings.
bellow	Those hogs **bellow** when they get mad.
final	Our **final** test in math is next Tuesday.
reply	Ben will **reply** to your letter this week.
throw	Nina can **throw** a ball 150 feet.
bright	The bulb in the desk lamp is **bright**.

Sort: Write each word from the Word Bank under the vowel sound it has.

long **i** spelled **y**

1. _____

2. _____

long **i** spelled **igh**

3. _____

4. _____

long **i** spelled **i**

5. _____

long **i** spelled **ie**

6. _____

long **o** spelled **oa**

7. _____

8. _____

long **o** spelled **ow**

9. _____

10. _____

Complete: Write the missing letters to spell each word from the Word Bank.

11. bell___ ___

12. tr___ ___d

13. fl___ ___t

14. repl___

15. br___ ___ ___t

16. sh___

17. thr___ ___

18. sl___ ___ ___t

19. sh___ ___l

20. f___nal

Solve: Write a word from the Word Bank to solve each riddle.

SPELLING BUILDER

Some words have unusual spellings for long **i**. **Height** and **buy** are two of these words.

21. I am the last one. After me, it's all over. _____

24. I am not brave when it comes to meeting others. _____

22. I am what you do with a ball when you pitch it. _____

25. I am hidden most of the time. I will sink a boat that runs into me. _____

23. A raft can do this. So can a tube. Can you? _____

26. I shine, I glow, I am a light in the night. _____

Choose: Write a word from the box to complete each sentence.

slight	reply	bellow	tried

27. Willy _____ to ride the old bike, but he could not.

28. When the bulls see us coming, they _____ and grunt.

29. There is a _____ echo when you speak in this room.

30. You must _____ to that letter by April 20.

Proofread: Read each sentence. Draw a line through the misspelled word. Write the correct spelling on the line.

31. The Bears tryed a trick on the final play of the game. _____

32. Do not let your raft flot near the shoal. _____

33. When Shelly made a bad throw, the kids in the stands let out a sligt groan.

_____

34. Ernie is too shye to reply to the new girl. _____

35. The bright light woke up Uncle Al and made him bello with rage!

_____

Write: Write a sentence to answer each question.

36. What is one odd food you have tried?

_____

37. How do you get set for a final test?

_____

LESSON 10   Long *a* and Long *e*

KNOW

■ Many patterns can stand for the long a sound besides a-Consonant-e.

■ The letters **ai** and **ay** can stand for long **a**.

■ Many patterns can stand for the long e sound besides **ee** and **ea**.

■ The letters **e**, **ey**, and **ie** can stand for long **e**.

Word Bank

Read each word in the Word Bank. Then read the sentence beside it.

faint	Too much sun can make you **faint**.
key	The big **key** will fit that lock.
stay	Your dog must **stay** out of the house.
brief	The coach gave a **brief** speech.
brain	To pass the test, you must use your **brain**.
legal	It is not **legal** to cross on a red light.
thief	A **thief** stole my CD pack.
even	Six is an **even** number.
payment	Shane used cash to make the **payment**.
alley	Latisha and her pals skate in the **alley**.

Sort: Write each word from the Word Bank under the vowel sound it has.

long a spelled **ai**	long a spelled **ay**	long e spelled **e**	long e spelled **ey**	long e spelled **ie**
1. _____	3. _____	5. _____	7. _____	9. _____
2. _____	4. _____	6. _____	8. _____	10. _____

Complete: Write the missing letters to spell each word from the Word Bank.

11. l___gal

12. st___ ___

13. k___ ___

14. br___ ___n

15. p___ ___ment

16. ___ven

17. all___ ___

18. br___ ___f

19. f___ ___nt

20. th___ ___f

Solve: Use words from the Word Bank to fill in the puzzle.

Across
- **23.** not a long time
- **26.** tiny street
- **27.** pass out
- **29.** not odd
- **30.** don't go away

Down
- **21.** means "okay by law"
- **22.** takes what is not his
- **24.** used to think
- **25.** made with cash or a check
- **28.** opens a lock

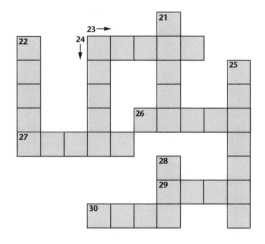

Proofread: Read each sentence. Draw a line through the misspelled word. Write the correct spelling on the line.

31. I must use my brane to find my key. _____

32. The theif ran into the alley. _____

33. Pam made a payment of ten dollars evin. _____

34. Kids stay on the dock for a breef time, and then they dive into the lake.

_____

35. Ari felt faynt when he found out that what he had done was not legal.

_____

Write: Write a sentence to answer each question.

36. What could make someone faint?

_____

37. What is the smallest even number?

_____

LESSON 11   Vowel Sounds /oi/ and /ow/

KNOW

- The /oi/ sound you hear in **coin** can be spelled **oi** or **oy**.
- The /ow/ sound you hear in **town** can be spelled **ou** or **ow**.

Word Bank

Read each word in the Word Bank. Then read the sentence beside it.

soil	Beets grow well in sandy **soil**.
crowd	The **crowd** shouted and clapped.
loyal	The boss thanked her **loyal** staff.
mound	Dolores hiked up the **mound**.
cloud	The sun went behind a **cloud**.
avoid	You should **avoid** those rickety steps.
prow	The **prow** of the boat bumped into the dock.
choice	You have a **choice** of milk or punch.
sound	I do not like the **sound** my car is making.
annoy	Bugs **annoy** us every night at dusk.

READING TIP

Notice the slashes around /oi/ and /ow/. The slashes before and after sounds show the sound but not the spelling.

Sort: Write each word from the Word Bank in the correct place.

/oi/ spelled **oi**	/oi/ spelled **oy**	/ow/ spelled **ou**	/ow/ spelled **ow**
1. _____	4. _____	6. _____	9. _____
2. _____	5. _____	7. _____	10. _____
3. _____		8. _____	

Complete: Write the missing letters to spell each word from the Word Bank.

11. ch____ ____ce

12. cl____ ____d

13. pr____ ____

14. s____ ____l

15. ann____ ____

16. m____ ____nd

17. cr____ ____d

18. l____ ____al

19. av____ ____d

20. s____ ____nd

Choose: **Complete each two-line poem by underlining the word that rhymes and makes sense.**

21. If I made a dive through a (cloud, prow),
22. I would be happy and (loyal, proud).

23. I stand proud on American (soil, choice).
24. You can count on me to be (annoy, loyal).

25. A dog sat on top of a (cloud, mound).
26. Its howl was a very sad (crowd, sound).

READING TIP

Is it long **o** or /ow/? The letters **ow** make the long **o** sound in words like **crow**. They make the /ow/ sound in words like **crowd**. When you come to a word with **ow**, look at all the letters and think about what word would make sense in that sentence. That will help you know whether to say long **o** or /ow/.

Choose: **Write a word from the box to complete each sentence.**

crowd	annoy	avoid	loyal

27. My kid sister hums just to _____ me.

28. You can sometimes lose a buddy in a _____.

29. A _____ pal will stand by you in bad times.

30. Stay on the path and _____ the mud.

Proofread: **Read each sentence. Draw a line through the misspelled word. Write the correct spelling on the line.**

31. Liz thinks the black clowd will drop rain on the soil. _____

32. Which men in the crowd are loial to the queen? _____

33. If you stand by the prow, avoyd the wet spots. _____

34. That grating sownd will annoy our pets. _____

35. As you pass the mound, you have a choise of trails. _____

Write: **Write a sentence to answer each question.**

36. What will a loyal pal do for you?

_____

37. What are two things that annoy you?

_____

LESSON 12   Long *u*

KNOW

■ The /o͞o/ sound you hear in **boot** can be spelled **ue, oo, u,** or **ew**.

■ The /yo͞o/ sound you hear in **few** can be spelled **ue, u,** or **ew**.

Word Bank

Read each word in the Word Bank. Then read the sentence beside it.

crew	Nora joined the **crew** of the red boat.
doom	A feeling of **doom** swept over the crowd.
tuna	That big fish is a **tuna**.
hue	Lime green is a bright **hue**.
pew	Herbie sat in the last **pew**.
ruby	Is that red stone a **ruby**?
spoon	You may eat the stew with a **spoon**.
human	Neil Armstrong was the first **human** on the moon.
true	The tale I will tell you is **true**.
music	That **music** has a cool beat.

Sort: Write each word from the Word Bank under the vowel sound it has.

/o͞o/ spelled **ue**	/o͞o/ spelled **oo**	/o͞o/ spelled **u**	/o͞o/ spelled **ew**
1. _____	3. _____	5. _____	9. _____
/yo͞o/ spelled **ue**	4. _____	6. _____	/yo͞o/ spelled **ew**
2. _____		/yo͞o/ spelled **u**	10. _____
		7. _____	
		8. _____	

Complete: Write the missing letters to spell each word from the Word Bank.

11. r___by

12. m___sic

13. cr___ ___

14. h___e

15. sp___ ___n

16. t___na

17. h___man

18. d___ ___m

19. p___ ___

20. tr___ ___

Neil Armstrong was the first human on the moon.

Solve: Write a word from the Word Bank to solve each riddle.

21. We make a boat go
When we row, row, row!

_____

22. You use me to eat
With your hand, not your feet!

_____

23. I am made with a flute
Or a trumpet that can toot.

_____

24. I'm the reddest bright thing
That can sit on a ring.

_____

25. I am brown, I am blue
I am green and black too.

_____

26. I'm a time of no hope,
When no one can cope.

_____

TECH TIP

Spell checking can help you with /o͞o/ and /yo͞o/. Words with the /o͞o/ sound or the /yo͞o/ sound are tricky to spell. When you use a computer word processor to write, be sure to spell check your work. This will help you find and fix any errors you made writing words with /o͞o/ or /yo͞o/ sounds.

Choose: Write a word from the box to complete each sentence.

true	human	tuna	pew

27. The film is based on a _____ tale.

28. Only a _____ can speak in sentences.

29. Ernesto sat in a _____ near the coat room.

30. Did you ask for a bun with _____ on it?

Proofread: Read each sentence. Draw a line through the misspelled word. Write the correct spelling on the line.

31. The sad musick gave us a feeling of doom. _____

32. The hue of a rooby is bright red. _____

33. A hueman can use a spoon to eat. _____

34. All the crew sat in the first pue. _____

35. Nori's tale of how he hooked that tewna is not true! _____

Write: Write a sentence to answer each question.

36. What kind of music do you like best?

_____

37. What is one way you can tell that a tale is not true?

_____

LESSON 13   Contractions

KNOW

- A **contraction** is made of two words put together.

- An **apostrophe** takes the place of one or more letters in a contraction.

- Some contractions are formed from **not**:
  did not → didn't

- Some contractions are formed from **is, are, was,** or **were**:
  she is → she's

- Some contractions are formed from **has, have,** or **had**:
  I have → I've

- Some contractions are formed from **will**:
  he will → he'll

Word Bank

Read each word in the Word Bank. Then read the sentence beside it.

it's	It's too late to go to the beach.
I've	I've seen that film six times.
she'll	She'll tell all her pals about this.
doesn't	Edwin **doesn't** like to play chess.
hasn't	The dog **hasn't** howled at all.
aren't	We **aren't** happy about the new rules.
we're	We're going to the lake on Friday.
didn't	I **didn't** take your pen or your pad.
wouldn't	A pal **wouldn't** play that kind of a trick.
you're	You're the first one in line.

Sort: Write each contraction from the Word Bank in the correct place.

formed from **not**	formed from **will**	formed from **is**
1. _____	6. _____	8. _____
2. _____	formed from **have**	formed from **are**
3. _____	7. _____	9. _____
4. _____		10. _____
5. _____		

Change: Write the contraction for each pair of words.

11. would not _____   **16.** has not _____

12. she will _____   **17.** I have _____

13. it is _____   **18.** you are _____

14. did not _____   **19.** does not _____

15. are not _____   **20.** we are _____

Choose: **Write a contraction from the box to complete each sentence.**

it's	she'll	doesn't	I've	didn't

21. Sherry says that _____ come to the play with me.

22. Last week our team _____ win any games.

23. I think _____ going to snow soon.

24. _____ asked you five times to pass the pepper.

25. Hamid _____ like roast beef, but he does like beef stew.

Choose More: **Write a contraction from the box to complete each sentence.**

hasn't	aren't	we're	wouldn't	you're

26. _____ you like a bite of my fudge?

27. The rain _____ stopped for three days.

28. We went to sports camp, and now _____ the best pitchers on our team.

29. The dogs _____ on the porch.

30. If _____ the last one to go, turn out the light.

Proofread: **Read each sentence. Draw a line through the misspelled word. Write the correct spelling on the line.**

31. Terry did'nt send that note. _____

32. I woudnt eat that meat if I were you. _____

33. Yo're not helping us at all! _____

34. It'is easy to catch a fish in this creek. _____

Write: **Write a sentence to answer each question. Use a contraction in each sentence.**

35. Did you swim to school today?

_____

36. Have you ever seen a horse fly?

_____

SPELLING BUILDER

Know the difference between **your** and **you're**. **You're** is the contraction for **you are**.

WRITING TIP

Make your writing sound real. Most people use contractions when they speak. So when you write dialog in a story, use contractions. It will make the talk sound a lot more real!

LESSON 14   Prefixes

KNOW

- A **prefix** is a word part that can be added to the beginning of some words.

- A prefix changes the meaning of the word to which it is added.

- The prefixes **un, dis,** and **mis** mean "not."

- The prefix **pre** means "before."

- The prefix **re** means "again."

Word Bank

Read each word in the Word Bank. Then read the sentence beside it.

preview	We saw a **preview** of a space chase film.
mistrust	I **mistrust** people who do not look at me when they speak.
unfair	It is **unfair** for some runners to get a head start.
refill	Will you **refill** the pitcher with water?
dislike	My sisters **dislike** bananas.
misplace	If you **misplace** your keys, you may not find them.
untangle	Please help me **untangle** this cord.
disconnect	Lucia will **disconnect** the lamp and then move it.
pregame	The coach made a **pregame** speech to the team.
refresh	A dip in the lake will **refresh** you.

Sort: Write each word from the Word Bank under its prefix.

un	dis	mis	pre	re
1._____	3._____	5._____	7._____	9._____
2._____	4._____	6._____	8._____	10._____

Complete: Write a prefix in each blank to spell a word that fits the definition.

11. _____like   *not like*

12. _____game   *before a game*

13. _____view   *an early look at*

14. _____tangle   *to get rid of tangles*

15. _____fresh   *to make fresh again*

16. _____fair   *not fair*

17. _____trust   *not to trust*

18. _____connect   *to unplug*

19. _____place   *to put in the wrong place*

20. _____fill   *to fill one more time*

Solve: Use words from the Word Bank to fill in the puzzle.

Across

23. to have no trust in
25. to make full again
26. to undo things that are connected

Down

21. to have no fondness for
22. to see early
24. not fair

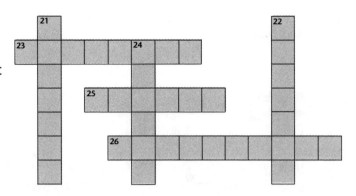

For many words you can create an antonym—a word with the opposite meaning—just by adding a negative prefix. Add **un** to **fair** and you create its antonym, **unfair**. Add **dis** to **like** and you create its antonym, **dislike**.

Choose: Write a word from the box to complete each sentence.

untangle	misplace	pregame	refresh

27. We will have a _____ feast of hot dogs.

28. If you _____ your glasses, someone may step on them.

29. A glass of limeade will _____ you.

30. Will you help me _____ this string?

Proofread: Read each sentence. Draw a line through the misspelled word. Write the correct spelling on the line.

31. It is unfair of you to disconect my phone. _____

32. Having seen the priview, I think I will dislike that film. _____

33. Fans sometimes missplace their tickets at pregame parties. _____

34. I misstrust a person who does not tell the truth. _____

35. Lex cannot untagle his laces. _____

36. Eliza will refill your glass, and the water will reefresh you. _____

Write: Write a sentence to answer each question.

37. What is one band or singer you dislike?

_____

38. What could make you mistrust a person?

_____

LESSON 15   Suffixes

KNOW

■ A **suffix** can be added to the end of a word. It changes the meaning of the word.

■ The suffix **ful** means "full of."

■ The suffix **less** means "without."

■ The suffix **en** means "made of."

■ The suffix **ish** means "relating to."

■ The suffix **ward** means "in the direction of."

Word Bank

Read each word in the Word Bank. Then read the sentence beside it.

careless	A **careless** camper can start a blaze.
harmful	Too many sweets can be **harmful** to your teeth.
wooden	We use **wooden** spoons to serve salad.
forward	When the light turns green, we will go **forward**.
childish	Stamping your boot is a **childish** thing to do.
golden	Those lemons have a **golden** hue.
endless	That film was so long that it seemed **endless**.
backward	If you run **backward**, you may bump into something.
selfish	Eating all the grapes yourself was **selfish**.
truthful	A witness must be **truthful**.

Sort: Write each word from the Word Bank under its suffix.

ful	less	en	ish	ward
1._____	3._____	5._____	7._____	9._____
2._____	4._____	6._____	8._____	10._____

Complete: Write a suffix in each blank to spell a word that fits the definition.

11. wood_____   *made of wood*

12. self_____   *greedy*

13. care_____   *sloppy*

14. child_____   *like a little kid*

15. truth_____   *does not lie*

16. gold_____   *gold-colored*

17. end_____   *going on forever*

18. for_____   *to the front*

19. harm_____   *something that harms*

20. back_____   *to the rear*

Label: Write a word from the Word Bank under each picture.

  STOP

21. _____ 22. _____ 23. _____ 24. _____ 25. _____

Choose: Write a word from the box to complete each sentence.

harmful	forward	childish	endless	truthful

26. Making sounds with a straw is _____.

27. The tale went on so long it seemed _____.

28. Nelson was _____ about how the glass got broken.

29. The troops marched _____.

30. Oil can be _____ to plants.

Proofread: Read each sentence. Draw a line through the misspelled word. Write the correct spelling on the line.

31. You can move that marker backward or foreward. _____

32. Would you prefer a goalden spoon or a wooden one? _____

33. Zandra was careless with the milk, but she was trutheful when we asked who spilled it. _____

34. Stepping on plants is childish and harmfull. _____

Write: Write a sentence to answer each question.

35. What is one way people are careless?

_____

36. Why is it good to be truthful?

_____

LESSON 16   Words for Workers

■ Some names for workers end with the /ûr/ sound. The /ûr/ sound can be spelled **er**. It can also be spelled **or**.

■ Some names for workers end with **ist**.

■ Some names for workers do not have special endings.

Word Bank

Read each word in the Word Bank. Then read the sentence beside it.

doctor	The **doctor** asked me to say "Ahhh!"
actor	The **actor** I like best plays a grandpa in that film.
teacher	Mario is good at math and wants to be a **teacher**.
painter	The **painter** must use a ladder to paint our house.
dentist	Did the **dentist** clean your teeth well?
clerk	I asked the **clerk** to help me find dish soap.
manager	My sister is the **manager** at the fast food stand.
nurse	A **nurse** cares for people who are ill.
coach	The **coach** showed the team a new play.
scientist	A **scientist** needs a lab to work in.

Sort: **Write each word from the Word Bank in the correct place.**

ends with **er**	ends with **or**	ends with **ist**	no special ending
1. _____	4. _____	6. _____	8. _____
2. _____	5. _____	7. _____	9. _____
3. _____			10. _____

Complete: **Write an ending in each blank to spell a word that fits the sentence.**

11. If you are the head of a shop, you are its manag_____.

12. If you treat people who are ill, you are a doct_____.

13. If you study the natural world, you are a scient_____.

14. If you paint homes, you are a paint_____.

15. If you are in a play, you are an act_____.

16. If you check teeth, you are a dent_____.

17. If you help people learn, you are a teach_____.

Solve: **Write a word from the Word Bank to solve each riddle.**

18. If you are ill, I might give you a pill. _____

19. To pay for something, come see me at the counter. _____

20. I'm not a doctor, but I am a healer. _____

21. If you're on the team, I'm in charge of you. _____

22. When homework is due, I collect it from you. _____

23. I use a drill with a lot of skill. _____

Choose: **Write a word from the box to complete each sentence.**

scientist	manager	actor	painter

24. A _____ is like a boss.

25. A _____ could make your home red or blue.

26. A _____ studies things in nature.

27. An _____ plays a role in a film.

Proofread: **Read each sentence. Draw a line through the misspelled word. Write the correct spelling on the line.**

28. Are you being treated by a docter or a nurse? _____

29. Our techer is the baseball coach. _____

30. Maria used to be a clurk, but now she is the manager. _____

31. That actor plays a mad sientist. _____

32. My dentist told the paintor to repaint the wall. _____

Write: **Write a sentence to answer each question.**

33. What kind of worker could you be now?

_____

_____

34. What kind of worker would you like to be someday?

_____

_____

TEST TIP

Many state tests ask you to use complete sentences when you write answers. To prepare for this, it's a good idea to write in complete sentences any time you take a test or quiz.

Part A

Complete: For each set, write a word from the list to complete each sentence.

bellow **A**
final
alley
payment

1. Renaldo crammed all night for the _____ test.
2. Lisa left her car in an _____.
3. An angry bull will _____ and paw the ground.
4. Cho made a _____ of fifty dollars.

loyal **B**
mound
music
crew

5. We will sing songs in _____ class.
6. A _____ is at work fixing the street.
7. A rabbit hopped to the top of the _____.
8. A _____ pal stands beside you.

it's **C**
we're
preview
refresh

9. A cold glass of water will _____ you.
10. I think _____ going to rain today.
11. The players yelled, "_____ the champs!"
12. The film _____ was thrilling.

forward **D**
selfish
doctor
scientist

13. The _____ did a study on Alaskan fish.
14. Taking all the best candy is _____.
15. Rita wants to become a _____ and help heal people.
16. Look out! That car is rolling _____!

Sort: For each set, write the words from the list in the correct place.

bellow **E**
final
alley
payment

long **a**	long **i**
17. _____	19. _____
long **e**	long **o**
18. _____	20. _____

preview **F**
forward
selfish
refresh

words with prefixes	words with suffixes
21. _____	23. _____
22. _____	24. _____

Complete: Write the missing letter or letters to spell each word. Look at the lists on page 44 if you need help.

25. self__ __ __   **33.** l__ __al
26. all__ __   **34.** for__ __ __ __
27. m__sic   **35.** m__ __nd
28. cr__ __   **36.** we'__ __
29. doct__ __   **37.** scient__ __ __
30. p__ __ment   **38.** f__nal
31. it'__   **39.** __ __fresh
32. bell__ __   **40.** __ __ __view

Proofread: Read each sentence. Draw a line through the misspelled word. Write the correct spelling on the line.

41. If those hogs bello, do not go forward. _____

42. Miki made the final paymant on her car yesterday. _____

43. A film cruw is at work in that alley. _____

44. Its time for the preview of next week's show. _____

45. Zoltan wants to be a doctor or a sceintist. _____

46. Molly is a loyal pal, but she can be seflish. _____

47. We'ere almost to the top of the mound. _____

48. A peach and some musick will refresh you and make you smile.

_____

Write: Write a sentence to answer each question.

49. When were you loyal to a pal?

_____

_____

50. When did you work as part of a crew?

_____

_____

Part B

Complete: **For each set, write a word from the list to complete each sentence.**

shoal   **A**
slight
brief
faint

1. I will go for a _____ run before lunch.
2. If you think you might _____, sit down.
3. Keep your boat away from the _____.
4. This egg has a _____ crack in it.

prow   **B**
avoid
doom
hue

5. Hot pink is a bright _____.
6. Don't let the _____ of the boat hit the dock.
7. You should _____ Main Street during its paving.
8. The unlucky hikers met their _____ in a cave.

she'll   **C**
wouldn't
mistrust
untangle

9. Let me help you _____ the rope.
10. Kylisha says _____ help us.
11. Melvin _____ forget to pick up his little sister.
12. I _____ the clerk with the big grin.

harmful   **D**
careless
manager
nurse

13. The _____ gave the workers a raise.
14. A _____ checked Jim's cuts.
15. Fumes from paint can be _____ .
16. If you are _____ with the paint, you will make a mess.

Match: **Draw a line from each word to its meaning.**

E
17. prow   • land just below the water
18. shoal   • one who cares for people who are ill
19. hue   • one end of a boat
20. nurse   • what pink, yellow, or red is

F
21. faint   • stay away from
22. mistrust   • get rid of knots
23. avoid   • become dizzy and fall
24. untangle   • have no faith in

CHAPTER 2 REVIEW

Solve: Use the words from the lists on page 46 to fill in the puzzle.

Across

26. not long
29. land just under the water
32. shade such as pale pink
33. not much
35. a kind of boss
37. helps a doctor
38. disaster

Down

25. one end of a boat
27. pass out suddenly
28. in a fast or sloppy way
30. have no faith in
31. get rid of tangles
34. not good for something
36. have no contact with

Proofread: Read each sentence. Draw a line through the misspelled word. Write the correct spelling on the line.

39. I misstrust the manager in that shop. _____

40. The wicked man will meet his doum soon. _____

41. A nurse cannot be carelles. _____

42. The ship must avoid the shole. _____

43. Tasha said sh'ell stop by for a brief visit. _____

44. I would'nt stand on the prow if I were you. _____

45. That hue has a slite hint of red. _____

46. If you feel fainte, sit down. _____

47. Those boots may be harmfull to your feet. _____

48. The manager will help you untangel the string. _____

Write: Write a sentence to answer each question.

49. Why is a nurse a helpful person?

_____

50. What is one thing you should avoid doing on a hike?

_____

LESSON 17   Words with the /ôr/ Sound or the /är/ Sound

KNOW

■ The /ôr/ sound you hear in the word **for** can be spelled **or, ore, oar,** or **oor**.

■ The /är/ sound you hear in the word **farm** can be spelled **ar** or **ear**.

Word Bank

Read each word in the Word Bank. Then read the sentence beside it.

score	Yasmin and Ella **score** points in almost every game.
floor	Andy spilled milk on the **floor**.
order	Mom gave Tim an **order** to clean up his room.
door	Shut the **door** on your way out.
forget	Did Ken **forget** to walk the dog?
board	We helped the teacher clean the **board**.
ignore	When my friend makes fun of me, I just **ignore** him.
party	Ruth baked a cake for the **party**.
garden	Pam likes to sit in the **garden**.
heart	Jogging is good for the **heart**.

Sort: **Write each word from the Word Bank in the correct place.**

/ôr/ spelled **or**

1. _____

2. _____

/ôr/ spelled **ore**

3. _____

4. _____

/ôr/ spelled **oar**

5. _____

/ôr/ spelled **oor**

6. _____

7. _____

/är/ spelled **ar**

8. _____

9. _____

/är/ spelled **ear**

10. _____

Complete: **Write or, ore, oar, oor, ar, or ear in each blank to spell a word that fits the sentence.**

11. The cat fell asleep on the fl_____.

12. Ben drew the shape of a h_____t in the sand.

13. Molly tried to ign_____ the boys.

14. The class had lunch in the g_____den.

15. We put our names on the b_____d.

16. Do not f_____get to brush your teeth.

Solve: Write a word from the Word Bank to solve each riddle.

17. I am in the classroom. You can write on me. _____

18. I pump your blood. _____

19. You must open me to get in. _____

20. You do this when you do not listen. _____

21. You do this when you do not remember. _____

SPELLING BUILDER

When you add **ed** or **ing** to a word in which the /ôr/ sound is spelled **ore**, don't forget to drop the **e**. For example, when you add **ing** to **score**, the correct spelling is **scoring**.

Choose: Write a word from the box to complete each sentence.

party	order	score	garden	floor

22. There are weeds growing in the _____.

23. Don't eat what has fallen on the _____.

24. The chief gave an _____ to his troops.

25. We were having so much fun, we forgot to keep _____ of the game.

26. We blew up balloons for the _____.

Proofread: Read each sentence. Draw a line through the misspelled word. Write the correct spelling on the line.

27. We will host a party in the gearden. _____

28. Did Kim oarder us to wipe the floor? _____

29. I could not see the score on the bord. _____

30. They never foreget to lock the door. _____

31. Do not ignor what you feel in your heart. _____

Write: Write a sentence to answer each question.

32. What is one good reason to have a nice garden?

_____

33. What is the best place to have a party?

_____

LESSON 18   Synonyms

KNOW

■ **Synonyms** are words that have similar meanings. For example, the word **chilly** is a synonym for the word **cold**.

Word Bank

Read each word in the Word Bank. Then read the sentence beside it.

decide	Shaily could not **decide** if she wanted to see the film.
chart	The teacher made a **chart** to show the new spelling rules.
sorrow	When the mayor died, the town was full of **sorrow**.
elegant	Her black dress was long and **elegant**.
choose	Mark had to **choose** a topic for his report.
graceful	That ballet dancer is very **graceful**.
diagram	The scientist used a **diagram** to show how computers work.
explore	I will **explore** my new school now.
search	I wanted to **search** the schoolyard for the note I had dropped.
sadness	The players felt **sadness** when they lost the game.

Sort: Use the Word Bank to write a synonym for each word below.

decide	explore	sadness	graceful	chart
1. _____	2. _____	3. _____	4. _____	5. _____

Complete: Write the missing letter or letters in each blank to spell a word that fits the sentence.

6. The weatherman looked at the ch____t and said that it would rain.

7. Let's go expl_____ the other side of the mountain.

8. Megan will d__cide where we will eat tonight.

9. The president's house was large and el__gant.

10. At the airport, a worker will s_____ch your bag.

11. Matt felt s__rrow because he could not go to the party.

12. I tried to be grace_____ as I walked onto the stage.

13. This d____gram shows how to put the table together.

14. The coach will ch____se the players for the game.

15. My family felt sad_____ when our trip was over.

Match: Draw a line from each word to its meaning.

16. diagram   • being unhappy

17. choose   • a chart that shows the parts of something

18. search   • moves with beauty

19. sadness   • to look for

20. graceful   • to select or pick

WRITING TIP

Use a variety of words when you write. Instead of using a word over and over in a paper, try replacing it with a synonym in some sentences. Your paper will sound a lot better!

Choose: Write a word from the box to complete each sentence.

decide	diagram	elegant	explore	sorrow

21. Our host was charming and _____.

22. This _____ shows how a bike brake works.

23. His _____ made it hard for him to smile.

24. Chuck had to _____ what to name the baby.

25. The kids wanted to _____ the forest.

Proofread: Read each sentence. Draw a line through the misspelled word. Write the correct spelling on the line.

26. The diagramm shows how corn grows. _____

27. Mason will chooze what color to paint the house. _____

28. The ice skater slowed down to make her moves look more graseful. _____

29. Tam felt sorroe when his pal moved away. _____

30. Julia couldn't deside if she wanted a cat or a dog. _____

31. I will surch that book for the answer. _____

Write: Write a sentence to answer each question.

32. What is one thing that would make someone feel sadness?

_____

33. What is one thing that is hard for you to decide?

_____

Words with the /ûr/ Sound

KNOW

■ The /ûr/ sound you hear in **turn** can be spelled **er**, **ur**, **ir**, or **ear**.

Word Bank

Read each word in the Word Bank. Then read the sentence beside it.

mirth	We felt **mirth** and joy as we watched the puppet show.
spurt	With a final **spurt**, Beth passed Tara and came in first.
shirt	Mom told me to tuck in my **shirt**.
sister	I like to read to my little **sister**.
heard	We **heard** a loud noise outside.
perhaps	**Perhaps** we will see some deer on our hike.
churn	We watched the waves **churn** and crash.
learn	What did you **learn** in science class today?
burst	The balloon may **burst** if you blow more air into it.
circle	The players ran around in a **circle**.

Sort: Write each word from the Word Bank in the correct place.

/ûr/ spelled **er**	/ûr/ spelled **ur**	/ûr/ spelled **ir**	/ûr/ spelled **ear**
1. _____	3. _____	6. _____	9. _____
2. _____	4. _____	7. _____	10. _____
	5. _____	8. _____	

Complete: Write er, ur, ir, or ear in each blank to spell a word that fits the sentence.

11. P____haps Kate will call next week.

12. John could not find his red sh____t.

13. The bag was so full that it b____st open.

14. I share a room with my sist____ .

15. David h_____d a door slam.

16. When I see a dog chase its tail, I feel m____th.

17. There is a c____cle in the center of the gym.

18. If you ch____n cream, you will make butter.

19. Jana will sp____t ahead on the last lap.

20. Would you like to l_____n how to do a backflip?

Match: Draw a line from each word to a word that means the same or almost the same.

21. perhaps   • joy

22. churn   • study

23. mirth   • swirl

24. burst   • maybe

25. learn   • explode

WRITING TIP

You can write easy rhymes. Many words in English have the /ûr/ sound in their final syllable. When you're writing a poem with rhyming lines, try ending a line with an /ûr/ word. You'll have a lot of choices for rhymes!

Choose: Write a word from the box to complete each sentence.

spurt	shirt	sister	heard	circle

26. That _____ has a spot on the pocket.

27. With a sudden _____ the plant grew tall.

28. We _____ a hissing noise from the tube.

29. Don't forget to _____ the date of my party.

30. Billy's _____ watches him when their mom and dad are out.

Proofread: Read each sentence. Draw a line through the misspelled word. Write the correct spelling on the line.

31. If the rain keeps falling, perhaps the dam will berst. _____

32. Ron wanted to learn how to chearn butter. _____

33. A spirt of water landed on my shirt. _____

34. The group was full of murth as they formed a circle and began dancing. _____

35. Carl herd his sister come home at 11 P.M. _____

Write: Write a sentence to answer each question.

36. What would you like to learn to make?

_____

37. What does your best shirt look like?

_____

LESSON 20   Antonyms

Word Bank

Read each word in the Word Bank. Then read the sentence beside it.

smooth	Lily found some **smooth** rocks by the river.
quiet	The street was empty and **quiet**.
defeat	**Defeat** came in the final seconds of the game.
shiny	The newly minted dime was very **shiny**.
rough	My hands are **rough** from working in the garden.
dull	After a few washings, the shirt faded to a **dull** green.
worthless	David likes to collect **worthless** things like bottle caps.
victory	The yells and clapping of the fans helped the team to **victory**.
noisy	It was **noisy** and crowded at the market.
priceless	That ruby is **priceless**.

Sort: Use the Word Bank to write an antonym for each word below.

dull	priceless	smooth	noisy	defeat
1. _____	2. _____	3. _____	4. _____	5. _____

Complete: Write the missing letter or letters in each blank to spell a word that fits the sentence.

6. Ben likes to read in a qu____t place.

7. The board was r_____ and needed to be sanded down.

8. Jill saw something sh__ny glittering in the water.

9. Mom frosted the cake with a creamy sm____th icing.

10. Our team will find a way to avoid def____t.

11. The lunch room is always crowded and n____sy.

12. The buckle on my belt has become d__ll.

13. This stamp has value, but that one is worth_____.

14. Don't let my little brother near that price_____ painting.

15. Two more points will give us a vict____y.

Match: Draw a line from each word to its meaning.

16. quiet   • the losing of a contest

17. smooth   • making little or no sound

18. victory   • the winning of a game

19. defeat   • having no bumps or nicks

20. worthless   • without value

Choose: Write a word from the Word Bank to complete each sentence. Think about the shape of each word.

21. Sasha found a ☐☐☐☐☐ penny on the ground.

22. It was a ☐☐☐☐ ride home on the dirt path.

23. The painting was a ☐☐☐☐☐☐☐☐ work of art.

24. The baby waved his ☐☐☐☐ rattle.

25. The apple looked ☐☐☐ until Maggie polished it.

Proofread: Read each sentence. Draw a line through the misspelled word. Write the correct spelling on the line.

26. The old kettle seemed dull next to the shiney new one. _____

27. This cream will make your ruogh hands feel smooth. _____

28. Alicia's two free throws turned defeet into victory. _____

29. The noizy bunch of kids made us wish for quiet. _____

30. My grandfather's watch may seem worthless to you, but it is pirceless to me. _____

READING TIP

Watch for contrasts. Sometimes authors use a pair of antonyms to show a difference. Stop and ask yourself, "Is the author telling me how two things are different?" Showing the differences between things is called **contrasting**. Noticing contrasts can help you get more out of what you read.

Write: Write a sentence to answer each question.

31. Where do you go to find peace and quiet?

_____

32. What is something that is priceless to you?

_____

LESSON 21   Homophones and Homographs

KNOW

■ Words that sound the same but have different spellings and meanings are called **homophones**.

■ Words that are spelled the same but have different meanings are called **homographs**.

Word Bank

Read each word in the Word Bank. Then read the sentence beside it.

soar	The glider will **soar** high over the land.
allowed	Running is not **allowed** on the pool deck.
creek	Little fish swim in that **creek**.
plain	Rula chose a **plain** scarf instead of a fancy one.
sore	Hal's arms were **sore** from loading boxes.
record	Our group will **record** a song on Tuesday.
aloud	The teacher read a funny story **aloud** to the class.
plane	Dan is learning to fly a **plane**.
creak	The stairs **creak** when anyone walks on them.
stern	Aisha's grandmother is a **stern** person.

Sort: Write the homophones from the Word Bank in pairs.

1. _____ and 2. _____   5. _____ and 6. _____

3. _____ and 4. _____   7. _____ and 8. _____

Now write the two words that remain. These words are homographs.

9. _____   10. _____

Complete: Write the missing letter or letters in each blank to spell a word that fits the sentence.

11. That old pl__n__ has two sets of wings.

12. You should not say al____d everything you think.

13. Jana has a s__r__ toe and can hardly walk.

14. Pl____n red paper will be fine for this gift.

15. Old houses often cr____k at night.

16. We put our things in the st____n of the boat.

17. Yelling is not all____ed in the halls.

18. Please keep a rec____d of the hours you work.

19. Bats s____r through the air after sunset.

20. My sister put a toy boat in the cr____k.

Solve: Use words from the Word Bank to fill in the puzzle.

Across
22. not fancy
25. small stream
27. fly high
28. okay to do

Down
21. you fly in this
23. so others can hear
24. hurting
26. a squeaky noise

TECH TIP

The spell checker on your computer won't notice if you use the wrong homophone. That's why you should proofread for spelling even when you use a spell checker.

Choose: Write a homograph from the box to complete each sentence.

record	stern

29. Carlene stands at the _____ of the boat to fish.

30. I will _____ your speech on this tape.

31. Do you have a _____ of how much you spent?

32. The leader seemed _____ and unfriendly.

Proofread: Read each sentence. Draw a line through the misspelled word. Write the correct spelling on the line.

33. No one is aloud to play in the creek. _____

34. If you read all your e-mail aloud, you will get a soar throat. _____

35. Andrew will reckord a thud and a creak for a scary film he is making. _____

36. Prem seemed sturn until he told a joke. _____

Write: Write a sentence to answer each question.

37. How late should students your age be allowed to stay up on a school night?

_____

38. Do you like plain things, or fancy ones? Why?

_____

LESSON 22   Long and Short *oo,* and *yoo*

KNOW

■ You hear the short **oo** sound in words like **foot, wood,** and **cookie**. It is spelled **oo**.

■ You hear the long **oo** sound in words like **hoop, true,** and **flute**. This sound is also called the long **u** sound.

■ The long **oo** sound can be spelled **oo, ue** or **u-Consonant-e**.

■ You hear the **yoo** sound in words like **value**. The **yoo** sound is often spelled **ue**.

Word Bank

Read each word in the Word Bank. Then read the sentence beside it.

chute	The **chute** slides trash to the trash cans.
tooth	That baby has only one **tooth**!
value	That large can of salsa is a great **value**.
spooky	At night, that house is **spooky**.
dune	A hill made of sand is a **dune**.
goodbye	She said **goodbye** to her friends after the party.
shook	When I met her, I **shook** her hand.
rescue	The workers will **rescue** that dog from the river.
proof	Jamal wanted **proof** that the printer had been fixed.
rookie	Is that player a **rookie**?

Sort: Write each word from the Word Bank in the correct place.

short **oo**	long **oo** spelled **oo**	long **oo** spelled **u-C-e**	**yoo**
1. _____	4. _____		9. _____
2. _____	5. _____	7. _____	10. _____
3. _____	6. _____	8. _____	

Complete: Write the missing vowels in each blank to spell a word that fits the sentence.

11. I need to see pr____f that the new key will work.

12. It was dark outside, and the forest looked sp____ky.

13. Eduardo found out that the baseball player was a r____kie.

14. It was easy for the camel to walk over the d__n__ .

15. At the end of the trip, Jessie said g____dbye to her brother.

16. We saw two films for the price of one, so the tickets were a good val____.

17. She was five years old when she lost her first t____th.

18. You need to throw that trash down the ch__t__ .

19. The workers will resc____ the cat that is stuck in the tree.

20. I did not agree with my friend, so I sh____k my head.

Match: Draw a line from each word to its meaning.

21. dune   • scary

22. spooky   • to save from danger

23. rescue   • a word to say farewell

24. rookie   • a hill of sand

25. goodbye   • a person new to a sport

SPELLING BUILDER

The word **tooth** does not form its plural in the usual way, by adding **s** or **es**. Instead, its spelling changes. The plural form of **tooth** is **teeth**. **Man, woman, mouse,** and **goose** are some other words that change spelling to form the plural. What are the plural forms of these words?

Choose: Write a word from the box to complete each sentence.

shook	tooth	proof	chute	value

26. The dog came out of the river and _____ its wet tail.

27. We cleaned up the kitchen and put the trash down the _____.

28. This _____ hurts when I eat ice cream.

29. The low price made the new car an amazing _____.

30. I used my student card as _____ of my age.

Proofread: Read each sentence. Draw a line through the misspelled word. Write the correct spelling on the line.

31. I hope that man can will rescyoo the swimmer. _____

32. Kenji said goodebye to the rookie. _____

33. By mistake, I threw my report down the chuet. _____

34. She did not want to walk along the spookey path to his house. _____

35. We met them at the door and shuke hands. _____

36. Toya wanted prufe that the stone was a real ruby. _____

Write: Write a sentence to answer each question.

37. How old were you when you lost your first tooth?

_____

38. What is one thing you have selected that was a good value?

_____

LESSON 23 Words with the /âr/ Sound or the /îr/ Sound

KNOW

■ The /âr/ sound you hear in **scare** can be spelled **are** or **ere**.

■ The /îr/ sound you hear in **steer** can be spelled **ear, eer, ere,** or **ier**.

Word Bank

Read each word in the Word Bank. Then read the sentence beside it.

weary	After walking to the store and back, Bob felt **weary**.
fierce	My new kitten acts very **fierce**.
peer	When a door is slightly open, people will **peer** into the room.
merely	She called it a mountain, but it was **merely** a hill.
spare	Maria had only one pencil with her, so she had none to **spare**.
sneer	The mean man had a **sneer** on his face.
warfare	**Warfare** had damaged the city and scarred the land.
sincere	His smile was big and **sincere**.
nowhere	The book was **nowhere** to be found.
wherever	**Wherever** Louis goes, his dog follows.

Sort: Write each word from the Word Bank in the correct place.

/âr/ spelled **are**

1. _____
2. _____

/âr/ spelled **ere**

3. _____
4. _____

/îr/ spelled **ear**

5. _____

/îr/ spelled **ere**

6. _____
7. _____

/îr/ spelled **eer**

8. _____
9. _____

/îr/ spelled **ier**

10. _____

Complete: Write are, ere, ear, eer, or ier in each blank to spell a word that fits the sentence.

11. Bobcats may look cute, but they are f_____ce animals.

12. The girls were busy, and couldn't sp_____ two hours for a film.

13. Mike goes wh_____ver he wants to go.

14. The twins sn_____ at people they think are not as cool as they are.

15. Naomi played baseball all day and is now w_____y.

16. Ivan is a good friend and gives sinc_____ advice.

17. The test had many questions, but it took me m_____ly twenty minutes.

18. The warf_____ in the area had spoiled the forest.

Circle: Circle the word that means almost the same as the bold word.

19. weary	near	warfare	sleepy
20. fierce	fun	mean	peer
21. sincere	truthful	spare	there
22. wherever	often	anyplace	always
23. merely	merry	only	nowhere

Choose: Write a word from the box to complete each sentence.

peer	warfare	sneer	nowhere	spare

24. I will _____ through that hole to watch the ball game.

25. A truck with a broken axle is going _____.

26. Jen has enough money for the bus and not a penny to _____.

27. When she saw her enemy fail, she wore a _____ on her face.

28. _____ had made it foolish to travel outside of the city.

Proofread: Read each sentence. Draw a line through the misspelled word. Write the correct spelling on the line.

29. His warm hug was sinceer. _____

30. A can of paint should be nowhare near an open flame. _____

31. She looks mean and fierce with that snere on her face. _____

32. Do you have a minute to sperr? _____

33. The test turned out to be mierly a quiz. _____

34. During warfare, you can be in danger whereever you go.

_____

Write: Write a sentence to answer each question.

35. What do you have to do that makes you feel weary?

_____

36. How do you feel when a friend is not sincere?

_____

LESSON 24   Words for the Computer

KNOW

■ Every syllable has a vowel sound. You can count the syllables in a word by listening to the number of vowel sounds.

■ Breaking words into syllables can help you spell them.

■ If you have trouble breaking a word into syllables, you can use the dictionary to find where the word splits.

Word Bank

Read each word in the Word Bank. Then read the sentence beside it.

software	That **software** will help you do your taxes.
Internet	Sharam found this map on the **Internet**.
modem	We have a **modem** so we can use the Internet.
document	Will you open that **document**?
digital	Scott has a **digital** picture of his dog.
display	Cory showed me her work on the **display** screen.
wireless	My mother's new telephone is **wireless**.
program	This computer **program** has a spell checker.
memory	Does that computer have enough **memory** to run this game?
gigabyte	This disk drive will hold a **gigabyte** of information.

Sort: Write each word from the Word Bank under the correct term.

two syllables   three syllables

1. _____   3. _____   6. _____   9. _____

2. _____   4. _____   7. _____   10. _____

                5. _____   8. _____

Complete: Write the missing syllable to spell a word that fits the sentence.

11. A picture you can send over e-mail is _____ital.

12. You need more mem__ry to install this software.

13. If you want to write, use a word processing _____gram.

14. This _____play shows what programs your computer has.

15. You can check the weather and your e-mail on the In_____net.

16. A computer that doesn't have a cord is wire_____.

17. A mo_____ will get you onto the Internet.

18. One giga_____ of memory can store a large amount of information.

Solve: Write a word from the Word Bank to solve each riddle.

19. It's a sure bet, I'll get you onto the Internet. _____

20. I'm not "hard" for you to use. I help you
write and play games, too. _____

21. You use me to check e-mail, or even learn how to sail. _____

22. If you have more words to write, open me up
to add to what you wrote last night. _____

23. I am a number for a lot of information. _____

24. Take me with you when you're bored.
I don't need a plug or cord. _____

Choose: Write a word from the box to complete each sentence.

digital	display	program	memory

25. Kavita opened the document and it came up on the _____.

26. This math _____ will help you study for the test.

27. The library computer needs a large amount of _____.

28. Tim changed the _____ picture by hitting a key.

**Proofread: Read each sentence. Draw a line through the misspelled
word. Write the correct spelling on the line.**

29. The modum doesn't work, so I can't
get onto the Internet. _____

30. The program didn't work because
there wasn't enough memorie. _____

31. As I typed, the words came up on the displaye. _____

32. I took my dijital camera to the party. _____

Write: Write a sentence to answer each question.

33. What kinds of things are wireless?

_____

34. What do you like to do on the Internet?

_____

*Cory uses the Internet to get
information for her report.*

Part A

Complete: For each set, write a word from the list to complete each sentence.

floor   **A**

heart

search

explore

1. Lou Ann gave her pal a _____ on Valentine's Day.
2. Will you help me _____ for my lost key?
3. The stone _____ was very hard and cold.
4. Lewis and Clark were sent to _____ the West.

heard   **B**

circle

noisy

quiet

5. That fan is so _____ that I can't sleep.
6. You can trace a dime to make a _____.
7. When I am alone, our home is _____.
8. I just _____ an odd noise outside.

plane   **C**

plain

rescue

shook

9. When Li _____ the punch, the top flew off and it spilled.
10. I need a ladder to _____ the cat in the tree.
11. We flew over the Grand Canyon in a small _____.
12. A _____ cake costs less than a fancy one.

fierce   **D**

nowhere

memory

digital

13. A _____ watch shows the time in numbers.
14. Your computer needs more _____ to run that program.
15. Tigers are _____ , but elephants are more powerful.
16. The chain came off my bike, so I am going _____.

Sort: For each set, write the words from the list in the correct place.

heard   **E**

nowhere

fierce

heart

vowel sound in **bird**		vowel sound in **peer**
17. _____	19.	_____
vowel sound in **fair**		vowel sound in **start**
18. _____	20.	_____

noisy   **F**

plane

quiet

plain

homophones		antonyms
21. _____	23.	_____
22. _____	24.	_____

Complete: Write the missing letter or letters to spell each word. Look at the lists on page 64 if you need help.

25. f__ __rce

26. pl__n__

27. h__ __ __d

28. expl__ __ __

29. resc__ __

30. pl__ __n

31. mem__ry

32. n__ __sy

33. h__ __ __t

34. sh__ __k

35. qu__ __t

36. fl__ __ __

37. nowh__ __ __

38. s__ __ __ch

39. c__ __cle

40. dig__tal

Proofread: Read each sentence. Draw a line through the misspelled word. Write the correct spelling on the line.

41. The plain flew in a circle over the ballpark. _____

42. Carla is training for serch and rescue work. _____

43. The room was so quiet I could hear my hart beat. _____

44. Olaf complained that there was nowear left to explore. _____

45. A digatle clock should not be noisy. _____

46. That computer has a lot of memery, but it's too plain for my taste. _____

47. I heard the roars of some fearce beasts. _____

48. When Lonnie shook the box, some parts fell to the flore. _____

Write: Write a sentence to answer each question.

49. What part of the world would you like to explore?

_____

_____

50. What is the most dramatic rescue you have seen?

_____

_____

Part B

ignore
garden
elegant
graceful

A

1. A deer is _____ in its movements.
2. Karla tried to _____ the noise from the dishwasher.
3. The new table made the dining room look _____.
4. Paulo planted tulips in his _____.

mirth
churn
worthless
priceless

B

5. The _____ paintings are locked in the safe.
6. We watched the waves _____ and surge.
7. This is not a jewel—it's a _____ bit of glass.
8. The rodeo clown spread _____ with his silly tricks.

sore
soar
chute
dune

C

9. The roofers threw trash down the _____.
10. My legs are _____ from riding my bike.
11. Luz climbed the _____ and looked out over the desert.
12. Hawks _____ and dive as they hunt for food.

sneer
warfare
software
document

D

13. Tanks and planes are used in _____.
14. This _____ lets me make graphs easily.
15. You should not _____ at a friend's efforts.
16. This _____ is proof that you own that car.

Match: Draw a line from each word to its meaning.

E

17. dune   • gladness
18. mirth   • hill of sand
19. garden   • channel leading down
20. chute   • area that has been planted

F

21. elegant   • pleasant-looking; showing good taste
22. worthless   • having no value
23. graceful   • having great value
24. priceless   • moving with smoothness

CHAPTER 3 REVIEW

Solve: Use the words from the lists on page 66 to fill in the puzzle.

Across
27. many battles
29. written information
33. without value
35. hurting
36. to fly high
37. pleasant-looking
38. a slide
39. a hill of sand
40. to mix and swirl

Down
25. full of flowers
26. worth lots and lots of cash
28. tells a computer what to do
30. not to look at
31. moving smoothly
32. a happy feeling
34. a look of no respect

Proofread: Read each sentence. Draw a line through the misspelled word. Write the correct spelling on the line.

41. I will ignore her snear. _____
42. That elagant gown must be priceless. _____
43. This document will put an end to the warfair. _____
44. Software that does not work is wurthless. _____
45. My hands are soar after I work in the garden. _____
46. Eagles are graceful when they sore. _____
47. Galya felt mirth as she slid down the shute. _____
48. We stood on a sand doon and watched the waves churn and crash. _____

Write: Write a sentence to answer each question.

49. In what sport do players make the most graceful movements?

_____

50. When do you feel mirth?

_____

CHAPTER 4

LESSON 25   Hard and Soft *c*

KNOW

■ The letter **c** can stand for the /k/ sound, as in the word **can,** or the /s/ sound, as in the word **rice**.

Word Bank

Read each word in the Word Bank. Then read the sentence beside it.

parcel	Mom sent me a **parcel** in the mail.
center	The bus stops in the **center** of town.
concert	Miguel performed in the spring **concert**.
cycle	We will **cycle** up the hill to visit Molly.
process	James is in the **process** of moving into a new home.
once	I want to walk on the beach just **once** before we leave.
peace	Clay likes the **peace** and quiet of the forest.
practice	To prepare for the game, the team will **practice** in the park.
vacation	Where did Paul go on **vacation**?
across	The kids swam **across** the lake.

Sort: Write each word from the Word Bank in the correct place.

c stands for /s/ sound	c stands for /k/ sound	c stands for both /s/ and /k/ sounds
1. _____	6. _____	
2. _____	7. _____	8. _____
3. _____		9. _____
4. _____		10. _____
5. _____		

Complete: Write the missing letter or letters in each blank to spell a word that fits the sentence.

11. Moss likes to pra____ti_____ his trumpet.

12. Put the flowers in the _____nter of the table.

13. Are you performing in the ____on_____rt this afternoon?

14. Mary sleeps in the room a_____oss the hall.

15. Where will you go on va_____tion this year?

Match: Write a word from the Word Bank next to its meaning. Think about the shape of each word.

16. ▭▭▭▭▭▭ steps followed to do or make something

17. ▭▭▭▭▭▭ a musical show or performance

18. ▭▭▭▭▭▭ a time of rest

19. ▭▭▭▭▭ a package or bundle

20. ▭▭▭ to ride a bike

Choose: Write a word from the box to complete each phrase.

center	once	peace	practice	across

21. _____ upon a time

22. _____ makes perfect

23. _____ and quiet

24. _____ of the earth

25. _____ the street

READING TIP

Is it /k/ or /s/? When the letter **c** appears before the vowel **a**, **o**, or **u**, it stands for the /k/ sound. When the letter **c** appears before the vowel **e** or **i**, it stands for the /s/ sound.

Proofread: Read each sentence. Draw a line through the misspelled word. Write the correct spelling on the line.

26. I took the parsel across the street. _____

27. We will practice before the consert. _____

28. Dad let us cykle once around the block. _____

29. Kevin hoped to find peece on his camping vacation. _____

30. They are in the prosess of constructing a skyscraper in the center of the city. _____

Write: Write a sentence to answer each question.

31. What is your dream vacation?

_____

32. What can you do to help promote peace?

_____

Compound Words

■ **Compound words** are made of two shorter words that have been put together. **Someone** and **playground** are compound words.

Word Bank

Read each word in the Word Bank. Then read the sentence beside it.

sunshine	The **sunshine** is so bright, it hurts my eyes.
backpack	Karla filled her **backpack** with books to bring to school.
something	I see **something** shiny on the pavement.
everyone	**Everyone** I know came to my party.
basketball	Sam can play **basketball** very well.
evergreen	**Evergreen** trees do not shed their leaves in the fall.
countryside	The **countryside** has many green hills and small farms.
wildflower	Cristina liked the smell of the **wildflower**.
understand	I can't **understand** Dan because he talks so fast.
highlight	The **highlight** of the play was the final song.

Build: Write each missing word or word part on the correct line.

1. under + stand = _____

2. some + _____ = something

3. _____ + shine = sunshine

4. wild + flower = _____

5. back + _____ = backpack

6. high + light = _____

7. _____ + side = countryside

8. every + _____ = everyone

9. basket + ball = _____

10. ever + _____ = evergreen

Complete: Write the missing word in each blank to spell a compound word that fits the sentence.

11. Basket_____ is a thrilling sport.

12. I will pick a _____flower to give to my friend.

13. That _____pack is too heavy to carry.

14. Nick did not under_____ the plot of the film.

15. My new shades keep the _____shine out of my eyes.

Solve: Write a word from the Word Bank to solve each riddle.

16. I am a very bright light that comes from the sky. _____

17. I am a sport that people play. _____

18. You can use me to carry books and things to school. _____

19. I am a place outside the city. _____

20. You can pick me from a field. _____

READING TIP

When you come to a long word you don't recognize, look to see if it is a compound word—a word made of two shorter words. If it is, you'll probably be able to read it easily by reading each part.

Choose: Write a word from the box to complete each sentence.

something	everyone	evergreen	understand	highlight

21. Can you _____ me if I speak in a soft voice?

22. Tell _____ at school to come to the pep rally.

23. The class trip to the zoo was the _____ of my day.

24. The _____ trees stay green all year long.

25. I have _____ important to ask you.

Proofread: Read each sentence. Draw a line through the misspelled word. Write the correct spelling on the line.

26. There is something very heavy in my backpak. _____

27. The countryside is full of evurgreen trees. _____

28. Ann's last shot was the hilight of the basketball game. _____

29. The red wyldflower looked bright in the sunshine. _____

30. I don't understand why evryone seems
to dislike running laps around the track. _____

Write: Write a sentence to answer each question.

31. What are some things you carry in your backpack?

_____

32. What is the highlight of your day at school?

_____

LESSON 27   Hard and Soft *g*

KNOW

- The letter **g** can stand for the /g/ sound, as in the word **give**, or the /j/ sound, as in the word **page**.

- The letter combination **dge** usually makes the /j/ sound.

Word Bank

Read each word in the Word Bank. Then read the sentence beside it.

badge	The police officer showed us her **badge**.
signal	The pilot will **signal** when it's time to prepare for landing.
gentle	A **gentle** breeze blew the sailboat to shore.
guess	I could not **guess** what was inside the box.
guard	Did the **guard** catch the thief?
figure	We saw a tall **figure** standing in the doorway.
bridge	Janice was afraid to look down while crossing the rope **bridge**.
village	Only twenty people still live in the **village**.
ravage	Winter storms **ravage** towns along the coast.
engine	The car **engine** needs to be checked.

Sort: Write each word from the Word Bank in the correct place.

words that have the /g/ sound

1. _____

2. _____

3. _____

4. _____

words that have the /j/ sound

5. _____

6. _____

7. _____

8. _____

9. _____

10. _____

Complete: Write the missing letters in each blank to spell a word that fits the sentence.

11. Marie has to do some shopping in the vill_____.

12. The class monitor gets to wear a yellow ba_____.

13. That horse in the stable is very _____tle.

14. Dad must drive across the bri_____ to get to work.

15. The sculptor made a fi_____re out of clay.

Match: Draw a line from each word to its meaning.

16. guess   • an outline or form

17. village   • soft or mild

18. figure   • to predict

19. ravage   • a small community

20. gentle   • to indicate

21. signal   • to destroy

READING TIP

Is it /j/ or /g/? The letter **g** often stands for the /j/ sound when followed by **i**, **e**, or **y**, as in **giraffe**, **gem**, and **gym**. The letters **dge** also often stand for the /j/ sound, as in **ridge**. The letter **g** often stands for the /g/ sound when followed by **a**, **o**, or **u**, as in **game**, **goat**, and **gust**.

Solve: Write a word from the box to solve each riddle.

badge	guard	bridge	engine

22. I watch and protect things. _____

23. You can drive or walk across me. _____

24. Police officers wear this. _____

25. I make a car go. _____

Proofread: Read each sentence. Draw a line through the misspelled word. Write the correct spelling on the line.

26. The car enjine broke down near a small village. _____

27. Gus is a very gentel puppy. _____

28. The gard showed us his badge. _____

29. John watched a small figure cross the brige. _____

30. Humans continue to ravadge the rain forest. _____

31. Did you singal the driver to pull over? _____

32. Can you gess who is at the door? _____

Write: Write a sentence to answer each question.

33. Do you think the job of crossing guard is important? Why or why not?

_____

34. Why is it important to be gentle with a baby?

_____

LESSON 28   More Homophones

KNOW

■ Words that sound the same but have different spellings are **homophones**.

Word Bank

Read each word in the Word Bank. Then read the sentence beside it.

made	Tatiana **made** a cake for my birthday.
weather	Last week the **weather** was warm and sunny.
through	Sandy couldn't see **through** the dirty window.
guessed	Rachel did not know the answer, so she **guessed**.
threw	Erika **threw** the ball to the catcher.
minor	Al was lucky that his injury was **minor**.
maid	The **maid** came yesterday and cleaned the house.
whether	I could not tell **whether** Minori had won the race.
guest	Theo's **guest** arrived at the house on time.
miner	The **miner** worked in a cave on the mountain.

Sort: Write the homophones from the Word Bank in pairs.

1. _____ and 2. _____   7. _____ and 8. _____

3. _____ and 4. _____   9. _____ and 10. _____

5. _____ and 6. _____

Complete: Write the missing letters in each blank to spell a word that fits the sentence.

11. The sand castle we m_____ was washed away by the waves.

12. I did not belong to the club, so I signed in as a g_____t.

13. The quarterback thr_____ the football as far as he could.

14. The m_____r used a pick to break the rocks.

15. Thalia g_____ed how many beans were in the jar.

16. Malcolm had a _____nor part in the play, and was not on stage for very long.

17. Our flight was cancelled because of the bad _____ther.

18. Their sister works as a m_____d in the city.

19. When I walked thr_____ the door, everyone yelled, "Surprise!"

20. We should find out whe_____ the museum is open.

Match: Draw a line from each word to its meaning.

21. maid   • someone you invite

22. through   • lesser in amount or importance

23. miner   • someone who cleans

24. minor   • in one side and out the other

25. guest   • someone who takes rocks from the earth

> **WRITING TIP**
>
> Don't be afraid to use a dictionary when you write a word that you know is a homophone and you aren't sure which spelling you should use.

Choose: Write a word from the box to complete each sentence.

whether	threw	guessed	made	weather

26. Fouad didn't have his watch, so he _____ that the time was two o'clock.

27. Jackie _____ the rope to her brother.

28. The players couldn't decide _____ the rules were fair.

29. The _____ was perfect for a picnic.

30. This car was _____ in Texas.

Proofread: Read each sentence. Draw a line through the misspelled word. Write the correct spelling on the line.

31. The guest came late because of the whether. _____

32. Could you tell weather she threw the ball to Sam or to me?

_____

33. She made the changes, but the difference was miner. _____

34. We could see through the window after the made had cleaned it.

_____

35. I guest that her dad worked as a miner. _____

Write: Write a sentence to answer each question.

36. What kind of weather do you like best? Why?

_____

37. What do you think would be the hardest part of working as a miner?

_____

LESSON 29   Final /əl/

KNOW

■ You hear the /əl/ sound in the last syllable of the words **little** and **pedal**.

■ The /əl/ sound can be spelled **al, el, il, ile,** or **le**.

Word Bank

Read each word in the Word Bank. Then read the sentence beside it.

label	Mimi looked for the sweater's **label**.
fertile	The corn grew tall in the **fertile** soil.
pencil	Use a **pencil** when you do your math homework.
medal	The ice skater from America won the gold **medal**.
puzzle	Jamir put together two pieces of the **puzzle**.
towel	Liza needed a **towel** when she got out of the pool.
normal	The sailors knew the heavy winds were not **normal**.
evil	That man may be mean, but I don't think he's **evil**.
hostile	The **hostile** guards would not let us pass.
cradle	Mom put the baby into the **cradle**.

Sort: Write each word from the Word Bank in the correct place.

/əl/ spelled **al**

1. _____
2. _____

/əl/ spelled **il**

5. _____
6. _____

/əl/ spelled **le**

9. _____
10. _____

/əl/ spelled **el**

3. _____
4. _____

/əl/ spelled **ile**

7. _____
8. _____

Complete: Write al, el, il, ile, or le in each blank to spell a word that fits the sentence.

11. Chloe did well in the contest and won a med_____.

12. Pedro spent all day working on the puzz_____.

13. Snow in June is not norm_____.

14. Use this tow_____ to dry the dishes.

15. Jenna rocked the baby to sleep in the crad_____.

16. The farmer always had crops to sell because his land was fert_____.

17. Sophie read the lab_____ to find out where the sauce was made.

18. The crowd was host_____ to the visiting team.

19. The teacher lost his pen so he used a penc_____.

Solve: **Write a word from the Word Bank to solve each riddle.**

TECH TIP

Watch out for the /əl/ sound. Since there are several spellings that stand for the /əl/ sound, use the spell check on your word processer to help you catch mistakes.

20. When you're wet, I'm what you try;
I help you to get dry. _____

21. It's time for math, don't use a pen;
I'm the one you use again. _____

22. I'm not too short, not too tall;
I'm not too big, not too small. _____

23. Use me to rock the baby to sleep;
do it soft so he won't weep. _____

24. Silver, bronze, even gold;
I'm given to winners who are bold. _____

25. I'm bad or wicked—that's me;
I'm something you should never be. _____

Choose: **Write a word from the box to complete each sentence.**

label	puzzle	fertile	hostile

26. I like to use a pencil on the crossword _____.

27. The yard always has weeds because of the _____ soil.

28. The _____ man looked as if he was ready to fight.

29. She read the_____ to find out how to clean the shirt.

Proofread: **Read each sentence. Draw a line through the misspelled word. Write the correct spelling on the line.**

30. I couldn't read the lable on the towel. _____

31. He won a medle for solving the puzzle without a pencil. _____

32. The country's ruler was hostil and evil. _____

33. The family settled in a valley where the land was fertal. _____

Write: **Write a sentence to answer each question.**

34. What should you be given a medal for?

_____

35. What kinds of puzzles do you like?

_____

LESSON 30 /k/ Spelled *ch*; /f/ Spelled *ph, gh*

KNOW

- The /f/ sound can be spelled **ph**, as in **photo**, or **gh**, as in **tough**.

- The /k/ sound can be spelled **ch**, as in **echo**.

Word Bank

Read each word in the Word Bank. Then read the sentence beside it.

anchor	The ship lowered its **anchor** near the rocky shore.
cough	Dust makes me **cough** and sneeze.
graph	The **graph** compared the sizes of the fifty states.
school	Tony learned about dinosaurs at **school**.
chorus	There are only female singers in the **chorus**.
telephone	We spoke on the **telephone** last night.
enough	Did you have **enough** to eat?
monarch	The queen served as **monarch** for ten years.
chrome	The **chrome** on the car bumper was shiny and new.
laugh	Tim and Jess had to **laugh** at the silly joke.

Sort: Write each word from the Word Bank in the correct place.

/k/ spelled **ch**	/f/ spelled **ph**	/f/ spelled **gh**
1. _____	6. _____	8. _____
2. _____	7. _____	9. _____
3. _____		10. _____
4. _____		
5. _____		

Complete: Write **ch, ph,** or **gh** in each blank to spell a word that fits the sentence.

11. The _____orus sang a song.

12. Please answer the tele_____one!

13. Did the comedy make you lau_____?

14. The monar_____ was kind to his subjects.

15. We get out of s_____ool at 3:15.

16. There is enou_____ food.

17. Ben had to make a temperature gra_____ for science class.

18. Tracy polished the _____rome on her father's car.

19. Divers found the an_____or at the bottom of the sea.

20. I tried not to cou_____ during her speech.

Circle: Circle the word that means almost the same as the bold word.

21. **laugh**   bath   giggle   run

22. **chrome**   metal   crisp   travel

23. **graph**   wild   fruit   chart

24. **monarch**   guard   coin   ruler

25. **enough**   plenty   empty   strong

Choose: Write a word from the box to complete each sentence.

| school | telephone | cough | anchor | chorus |

26. Mary stayed after _____ to study.

27. You won't _____ after taking this cold medicine.

28. My mom sang in the town _____.

29. Alex called me on the _____ early yesterday.

30. The ship's captain told the crew to drop the _____.

Proofread: Read each sentence. Draw a line through the misspelled word. Write the correct spelling on the line.

31. The ship's new anker shined like it was made of chrome.

   _____

32. Paul sang in the corus at school. _____

33. I think the monark has enough power. _____

34. David would couph so strangely that I had to laugh. _____

35. He will explain the graff over the telephone. _____

Write: Write a sentence to answer each question.

36. What kinds of jokes make you laugh the most?

   _____

37. What is your favorite subject at school? Why?

   _____

The word **graph** comes from a Greek root meaning "to write." Knowing this can help you figure out other words like **telegraph, photograph,** and **autograph**. Whose autograph would you like to have?

LESSON 31   Words for Geography

KNOW

- Breaking long words into syllables can help you spell them.

- Every syllable has a vowel sound. You can count the syllables in a word by listening to the number of vowel sounds.

- A first syllable that has the Consonant-Vowel-Consonant (CVC) pattern often has a short vowel sound.

- A first syllable that has the Consonant-Vowel pattern often has a long vowel sound.

Word Bank

Read each word in the Word Bank. Then read the sentence beside it.

climate	Hannah is used to living in a cold **climate**.
rainfall	The town gets less than two inches of **rainfall** each year.
continent	Few animals can survive on the **continent** of Antarctica.
hemisphere	China is a country in the Northern **Hemisphere**.
latitude	**Latitude** lines run east and west on a map.
longitude	**Longitude** lines run north and south on a map.
current	The raft was swept downstream by the strong **current**.
landform	A bluff is a kind of **landform**.
elevation	Hiking at a higher **elevation** made Kate dizzy.
equator	The **equator** divides the earth into two hemispheres.

Sort: Write each word from the Word Bank under the correct term.

two syllables	three syllables	four syllables
1. _____	5. _____	10. _____
2. _____	6. _____	
3. _____	7. _____	
4. _____	8. _____	
	9. _____	

READING TIP

Sometimes finding a shorter word you know in a longer word can help you read the longer word. But this doesn't always work, as is the case with **mate** in **climate** and **long** in **longitude**.

Complete: Write the missing letters in each blank to spell a word that fits the sentence.

11. The closer you are to the e_____tor, the hotter it gets.

12. This city has a mild _____mate.

13. The comet can only be seen in the Northern Hemis_____.

14. Tiffany hopes to travel around the con_____nent of Africa.

15. We will go where the cur_____ takes us.

Label: Write a word from the Word Bank for each picture on the right.

16. _____

17. _____

18. _____

19. _____

20. _____

21. _____

16.

17.

Solve: Write a word from the box that fits each clue.

| climate | rainfall | current | landform |

22. I am water that moves steadily in one direction. _____

23. I tell about the usual types of weather in one place. _____

24. I am land that has a shape of some kind. _____

25. I am the amount of water that falls in one place during a period of time. _____

18.

19.

Proofread: Read each sentence. Draw a line through the misspelled word. Write the correct spelling on the line.

26. Any point on the equater has a latitude of zero degrees.

_____

27. The higher the elevation, the colder the climat gets. _____

28. Heavy rainfall can make the currant of a river stronger.

_____

29. It is winter in the Northern Hemisphear. _____

20.

Write: Write a sentence to answer each question.

30. What is the climate like in your area?

_____

31. Would you like to visit a place on the equator? Why or why not?

_____

21.

LESSON 32   Words for Government

KNOW

- Breaking long words into syllables can help you spell them.

- Every syllable has a vowel sound. You can count the syllables in a word by listening to the number of vowel sounds.

- If you have trouble breaking a word into syllables, use a dictionary to find where the word splits.

Word Bank

Read each word in the Word Bank. Then read the sentence beside it.

president	The **president** gave an important speech about his goals.
senator	A **senator** represents people from his or her state.
representative	Each district elects a **representative** to send to the capital.
congress	The members of **congress** meet to discuss and pass laws.
court	A **court** hears cases and makes judgments based on the law.
justice	A Supreme Court **justice** is appointed by the President.
election	The **election** for student body president will be close.
majority	It takes a **majority** of votes to win the election.
government	The **government** of a country makes its laws and rules.
federal	The **federal** government is divided into three branches.

Sort: Write each word from the Word Bank under the correct term.

one syllable

1. _____

two syllables

2. _____

3. _____

three syllables

4. _____

5. _____

6. _____

7. _____

8. _____

four syllables

9. _____

five syllables

10. _____

Complete: Write the missing syllable to spell a word that fits the sentence.

11. The majori_____ of students voted in the last election.

12. The new sen____tor gave a great speech to her supporters.

13. Each class will send a representa_____ to the meeting.

14. Today _____gress will debate a bill.

15. The _____ident meets with leaders from other countries this week.

16. A Supreme Court jus_____ may retire this year.

17. Every vote counts in the spring elec_____.

Match: Draw a line from each word to its meaning.

18. court   ● an event in which people vote to choose someone for a job in a government

19. majority   ● someone who serves on a court

20. justice   ● the leader of a particular type of government

21. election   ● one of two elected representatives from each state

22. president   ● a place where disputes are heard and judgments are made

23. senator   ● a number at least one more than half

Choose: Write a word from the box to complete each sentence.

representative	congress	federal	government

24. Nina wants to be her school's _____ at the state meeting.

25. Mr. Watson teaches about how our system of _____ works.

26. The members of _____ worked hard to get elected.

27. The President is head of the _____ government.

Proofread: Read each sentence. Draw a line through the misspelled word. Write the correct spelling on the line.

28. The elderly justise has been on the court for fifty years. _____

29. The president favors a new federel law promising more jobs for workers. _____

30. Hattie Caraway was the first female senater elected to the U.S. government. _____

Write: Write a sentence to answer each question.

31. Who are the two senators from your state?

_____

32. Do you think you might like to serve in the government someday? Why or why not?

_____

The White House is the home of the President of the United States.

Part A

Complete: For each set, write a word from the list to complete each sentence.

peace   **A**
vacation
sunshine
something

1. Danny found _____ to keep him busy.
2. Where can I go to find some _____ and quiet?
3. I wore a visor because the _____ was bright.
4. After working so hard, you need a _____!

gentle   **B**
bridge
weather
whether

5. It took a year to build the _____ across the river.
6. I'm not sure _____ I will go to the game.
7. I hope the _____ is nice at the beach.
8. Greg had to be very _____ with the tiny kitten.

label   **C**
cradle
chorus
enough

9. Emily sings in the _____.
10. You can find out by reading the _____ on the box.
11. We have _____ time to get to the theater.
12. How long has the baby been asleep in his _____?

current   **D**
longitude
president
representative

13. Her district chose her as its _____ in Congress.
14. The _____ of a city shows how far north or south of the equator it is.
15. The _____ is slower where the river is wide.
16. George Washington was elected _____.

Sort: For each set, write the words from the list in the correct place.

enough   **E**
chorus
peace
gentle

/s/ spelled c		/j/ spelled g
17. _____	19.	_____
/f/ spelled **gh**		/k/ spelled **ch**
18. _____	20.	_____

sunshine   **F**
weather
something
whether

homophones		compound words
21. _____	23.	_____
22. _____	24.	_____

Complete: Write the missing letter or letters to spell each word.
Look back at the lists on page 84 if you need help.

25. pres__dent

26. pea__e

27. cu__ __ent

28. s__nshine

29. __ __orus

30. bri__ge

31. lab__l

32. wea__ __er

33. wh__ther

34. cradl__

35. __entle

36. enou__ __

37. someth__ng

38. long__tude

39. vac__tion

40. represent__tive

Proofread: Read each sentence. Draw a line through the misspelled
word. Write the correct spelling on the line.

41. Sam took a long vacation to get some pease and quiet. _____

42. The president told the crowd that he had somthing
new planned for his second term. _____

43. The bad whether forced the ship to veer south by
two degrees longitude. _____

44. A lable on the map shows where the river's
current is strongest. _____

45. When the baby has had enough milk, put her
to bed in the cradel. _____

46. I don't know whether I'll join the corous. _____

47. We had a full day of sunshine with a jentle breeze. _____

48. Our representative is trying to get money
for a new bridge. _____

Write: Write a sentence to answer each question.

49. What is the first thing you would do if you became President of the
United States?

_____

_____

50. What is your least favorite kind of weather?

_____

_____

Part B

Complete: For each set, write a word from the list to complete each sentence.

parcel **A**
process
countryside
highlight

1. Exploring the ruins was the _____ of my trip.
2. Tito went biking in the _____.
3. This _____ came in the mail yesterday.
4. Fixing your car can be a difficult _____.

figure **B**
engine
through
threw

5. She _____ the ball harder than anyone else.
6. Please hand the boxes _____ the open window.
7. There's a problem with our car's _____.
8. I could barely make out the _____ by the road.

hostile **C**
fertile
monarch
graph

9. He created a _____ showing the town's population growth.
10. The river valley was a _____ area for crops.
11. Cam acted in a _____ way throughout the trip.
12. Queen Elizabeth II has been England's _____ since 1952.

climate **D**
hemisphere
justice
government

13. He has been a _____ on the Supreme Court for 20 years.
14. West Texas has a very hot and dry _____.
15. The _____ passes laws and sets taxes.
16. Australia lies entirely in the Southern _____.

Match: Draw a line from each word to its meaning.

E
17. parcel   • good for plants to grow in
18. monarch   • half of the earth
19. fertile   • a package
20. hemisphere   • the supreme ruler of a country

F
21. hostile   • the usual weather that occurs in a place
22. climate   • unfriendly
23. engine   • a member of the U.S. Supreme Court
24. justice   • the motor that moves a machine

Solve: Use the words from the lists on page 86 to fill in the puzzle.

Across
26. in one side and out the other
31. king or queen
33. machine motor
34. good for growing plants
36. form; shape
38. the Northern _____
39. long-term weather
40. mean; angry

Down
25. tossed
27. the best part
28. rural area
29. chart, table, _____
30. Supreme Court member
32. system of rule
35. something wrapped up or packaged
37. method; operation

Proofread: Read each sentence. Draw a line through the misspelled word. Write the correct spelling on the line.

41. A democracy is a government that has no monark. _____

42. This graff shows changes in climate. _____

43. The walk in the countryside was the highlite of my day. _____

44. She was hostile to the Supreme Court justiss. _____

45. The gas goes through the tube to the enjin. _____

46. He through rocks to keep the crows away from the fertile fields. _____

47. Making the clay figure was a long proses. _____

48. The parcel was mailed in the Southern Hemisfere. _____

Write: Write a sentence to answer each question.

49. What is the highlight of your week so far?

_____

50. Would you make a good Supreme Court justice? Why or why not?

_____

CHAPTER 5

LESSON 33   Endings -*ion, -sion, -tion*

KNOW

■ The endings **ion, sion,** and **tion** are suffixes that can turn verbs into nouns.

■ The endings **ion, sion,** and **tion** are often pronounced /shən/. You hear this sound in the last syllable of the word **action.**

Word Bank

Read each word in the Word Bank. Then read the sentence beside it.

expression	His smile was an **expression** of his joy.
fashion	Iris likes **fashion** and makes her own clothes.
champion	By winning the game, Martin became the new **champion.**
vision	The nurse wore glasses to correct her **vision.**
permission	May I have **permission** to leave early?
promotion	The clerk worked hard and got a **promotion.**
caution	You should use **caution** when running in the rain.
persuasion	Rory used his powers of **persuasion** to talk me into coming.
sensation	I touched the snow and felt a cold **sensation.**
action	The story was slow and did not have much **action.**

Sort: Look at the letters at the end of each word in the Word Bank. Then write the word on the correct line.

ion	tion	sion	ssion
1. _____	3. _____	7. _____	9. _____
2. _____	4. _____	8. _____	10. _____
	5. _____		
	6. _____		

Complete: Write **ion, tion, sion,** or **ssion** in each blank to spell a word that fits the sentence.

11. After the loss, his face wore a sad expre_____.

12. Paige earned a promo_____ to editor of the sports page.

13. Please use cau_____ when swimming in the ocean.

14. Erica was the champ_____.

15. The fast ride gave us the sensa_____ of flying.

16. The doctor tested my vi_____ and hearing.

17. The coach showed us the ac_____ of swinging a bat.

18. That style is in fash_____.

19. Cole needs permi_____ to go on the trip.

20. When asking didn't work, the students tried persua_____.

Circle: Circle the word that means almost the same as the bold word.

VOCABULARY BUILDER

Many words with the endings **ion**, **sion**, or **tion** belong to families of related words. Knowing the meaning of one word in the family (like **sensation**) can help you figure out other words (**sense, sensible, sensitive, sensory, sensual**).

21. champion   weak   winner   animal

22. vision   hearing   spot   sight

23. sensation   feeling   soft   sink

24. action   sleep   dull   movement

25. fashion   quick   style   fall

Choose: Write a word from the box to complete each sentence.

caution	permission	promotion	persuasion	expression

26. Javier could not go because his _____ slip was not signed.

27. I thought that _____ would change her mind.

28. The yellow sign means we should move with _____.

29. The man's angry _____ showed that he was hostile.

30. My job became harder after my _____.

Proofread: Read each sentence. Draw a line through the misspelled word. Write the correct spelling on the line.

31. Our vision in the fog was poor, so we drove with caushion. _____

32. After the fasion show, Thandie got a promotion. _____

33. Nick used persuasion to gain permision. _____

34. At the game, we watched the champion in acshun. _____

35. The painful expreshion on her face was the result of a burning sensation on her arm. _____

Platform boots are a fashion you may choose to wear with caution.

Write: Write a sentence to answer each question.

36. In what sport or activity would you like to be a champion?

_____

37. What is one trend in fashion today that you think is not a good idea?

_____

LESSON 34   Final /ən/

KNOW

■ Many words that end in **an, en, in, on,** or **ain** contain the /ən/ sound you hear at the end of **human, kitchen, cabin, person,** and **fountain.**

Word Bank

Read each word in the Word Bank. Then read the sentence beside it.

urban	Margaret grew up in an **urban** area.
proven	You have **proven** your ability to ride a horse.
raisin	Dylan found a **raisin** in his pocket.
wagon	I pulled my sister to the park in a small, red **wagon.**
curtain	Joan asked me to close the **curtain.**
veteran	Marcy was a **veteran** basketball player.
mountain	We will camp at the bottom of the **mountain.**
frighten	Don't **frighten** the birds away.
cousin	I will pick up my **cousin** at the airport.
reason	Ikuko has a good **reason** for being late.

Sort: Write each word from the Word Bank in the correct place.

ends in /ən/ spelled **an**

1. _____

2. _____

ends in /ən/ spelled **en**

5. _____

6. _____

ends in /ən/ spelled **in**

9. _____

10. _____

ends in /ən/ spelled **on**

3. _____

4. _____

ends in /ən/ spelled **ain**

7. _____

8. _____

Complete: Write the missing letters in each blank to spell a word that fits the sentence.

11. It took the hikers three days to reach the top of the mount_____.

12. If you are too loud, you will fright_____ the animals.

13. Did Jason give a reas_____ for quitting the team?

14. Ryan is my cous_____ , not my brother.

15. Do you sleep with the curt_____ open?

Match: Write a word from the Word Bank next to its meaning. Think about the shape of each word.

16. ⬚⬚⬚⬚⬚⬚ a child of one's aunt or uncle

17. ⬚⬚⬚ having to do with, or located in, a city

18. ⬚⬚⬚⬚ a small cart with wheels

19. ⬚⬚⬚⬚⬚⬚ a dried grape

20. ⬚⬚⬚⬚⬚⬚ a person with experience in an activity or job

Choose: Write a word from the box to complete each sentence.

proven	curtain	mountain	frighten	reason

21. Dana opened the _____ in her bedroom.

22. The thunderstorm is sure to _____ the kids.

23. There is no _____ to get so angry.

24. Edward has _____ himself to be a true friend.

25. There is snow on the peak of the _____.

VOCABULARY BUILDER

Just add the suffix **en** to many words to make verbs (action words). For example, add **en** to **fright** to make **frighten**, and **en** to **cheap** to make **cheapen**.

Proofread: Read each sentence. Draw a line through the misspelled word. Write the correct spelling on the line.

26. My cousen loves to bake raisin bread. _____

27. The quarterback has proven that he can play like a veteren. _____

28. That dark shadow on the curtain may frightin the baby. _____

29. Seth pulled the wagon up the mountin. _____

30. Urben traffic is one reason some people move out of the city. _____

Write: Write a sentence to answer each question.

31. What kinds of things frighten people?

_____

32. What are some benefits of living in an urban location?

_____

LESSON 35   The Schwa Sound in the First or Second Syllable

KNOW

■ The /ə/ sound you hear at the beginning of **about** and in the middle of **acrobat** can be spelled **a, e,** or **o**.

Word Bank

Read each word in the Word Bank. Then read the sentence beside it.

again	If you do not succeed the first time, try **again**.
acrobat	The **acrobat** twisted and twirled in the air.
commute	Betty has to **commute** to work every day.
itemize	You must **itemize** all of the shop's goods on a list.
oblige	The piano player will **oblige** our request for another song.
above	The upstairs bedroom is **above** the kitchen.
magazine	There is a good story in the latest issue of that **magazine**.
career	Mike has made a lot of money in his business **career**.
gasoline	Your car is almost out of **gasoline**!
ceramic	The **ceramic** jar fell to the floor and broke into pieces.

Sort: Write each word from the Word Bank in the correct place.

/ə/ spelled **a**	/ə/ spelled **e**	/ə/ spelled **o**
1. _____	5. _____	7. _____
2. _____	6. _____	8. _____
3. _____		9. _____
4. _____		10. _____

Complete: Write the missing letter in each blank to spell a word that fits the sentence.

11. There is always heavy traffic during my afternoon c__mmute.

12. I am not sure how to it__mize things on my tax forms.

13. Paula will never beat me __gain!

14. My grandma had a long c__reer in politics.

15. Stan read about the animal in a nature mag__zine.

16. The key is __bove the door.

17. The acr__bat carefully balanced on the tightrope.

18. The price of gas__line makes it expensive to fill up your car.

19. The team leader found a c__ramic pot that is over 2,000 years old!

20. I cannot __blige your demands.

Solve: Use words from the Word Bank to fill in the puzzle.

Across
22. monthly publication
23. to list each item
24. life's work
26. high-flying gymnast
29. to satisfy or serve
30. to go back and forth to work

Down
21. fuel
25. made from baked clay
27. once more
28. over or atop

TECH TIP

Since the /ə/ sound can be spelled with several different letters, you may be unsure of the correct spelling of a word with /ə/. Take a moment to use the spell checker on your word processor to check the word—you may be glad you did!

Choose: Write a word from the box to complete each sentence.

| above | magazine | itemize | again | commute |

31. Darren read a _____ while he waited at the office.

32. When no one answered, I pressed the doorbell _____.

33. Gavin has to _____ an hour each way to and from work.

34. The jet flew high _____ the mountains.

35. The intern must _____ the new artifacts that have been given to the museum.

Proofread: Read each sentence. Draw a line through the misspelled word. Write the correct spelling on the line.

36. The acrobat will ablige the crowd's request for another flying flip.

_____

37. I only commute when my car has plenty of gasiline. _____

38. Please hang that painting obove the stairs again. _____

Write: Write a sentence to answer each question.

39. What career would you like to pursue when you get older?

_____

40. What is your favorite magazine?

_____

LESSON 36   More Prefixes

KNOW

■ A **prefix** is a word part that can be added to the beginning of some words.

■ A prefix changes the meaning of the word to which it is added.

■ The prefix **anti** means "against."

■ The prefix **auto** means "self."

■ The prefix **co** means "together."

■ The prefix **inter** means "between."

■ The prefix **sub** means "below."

Word Bank

Read each word in the Word Bank. Then read the sentence beside it.

antiwar	The **antiwar** group organized a march.
submarine	Will looked over the side of the boat and saw a **submarine**!
cooperate	Our team won't do well unless we **cooperate**.
interrupt	If you save your questions until the end, you won't have to **interrupt** the speaker.
automatic	That light is on an **automatic** timer.
coordinate	Can you **coordinate** the club meetings?
interview	Ari got the job because his **interview** went well.
automobile	The red car wouldn't work, so Amy drove the blue **automobile**.
antibody	The shot made his blood produce the **antibody**.
submerge	We watched the divers **submerge** themselves in the river.

Sort: Write each word from the Word Bank under its prefix.

anti	auto	co	inter	sub
1. _____	3. _____	5. _____	7. _____	9. _____
2. _____	4. _____	6. _____	8. _____	10. _____

Complete: Write a prefix in each blank to spell a word that fits the definition.

11. _____mobile   *a vehicle that propels itself*

12. _____merge   *to put under water*

13. _____ordinate   *to arrange together*

14. _____war   *against war*

15. _____marine   *a ship that can go under the water*

16. _____operate   *to work together*

17. _____matic   *acting or working by itself*

18. _____rupt   *to stop an action by breaking in on it*

Solve: Write a word from the Word Bank to solve each riddle.

19. I get upset when people fight;
Peace is what I think is right. _____

20. This ship can take you beneath the sea
To travel with the fishes swimming free. _____

21. It takes you places near and far;
Another name for it is "car." _____

22. Breaking in on something on the go,
People do this and stop the flow. _____

23. I'm in your blood to help you fight.
I work against sickness day and night. _____

24. When you want a job, I'm what you do;
I'm the way a boss can get to know you. _____

READING TIP

When you recognize a prefix in a word, you also know the beginning syllable or syllables in that word. For example, the first syllable in **submerge** is **sub** and the first two syllables in **interview** are **in** and **ter**.

Choose: Write a word from the box to complete each sentence.

submerge	cooperate	automatic	coordinate

25. Everyone had to _____ days off so we could meet together.

26. No one needs to set the alarm because it is _____.

27. If we want to move this table, we must _____ with each other!

28. Lucinda had to _____ the shirt in soapy water to get the stain out.

Proofread: Read each sentence. Draw a line through the misspelled word. Write the correct spelling on the line.

29. Carmen has an inturview for a job to sell automobiles. _____

30. Every time I try to coordinate the group,
someone interupts me! _____

31. The scientists had to coperate to find the antibody. _____

Write: Write a sentence to answer each question.

32. What kind of automobile would you like to own? Why?

_____

33. When is it okay to interrupt someone?

_____

LESSON 37   More Suffixes

KNOW

■ A **suffix** is a word part that can be added to the end of a word. It changes the meaning of the word.

■ The suffix **logy** means "the science or study of."

■ The suffix **ic** means "relating to."

■ The suffix **ate** means "characterized by."

■ The suffix **ism** can mean "the quality of" or "the system of."

■ The suffix **ness** means "the quality of."

Word Bank

Read each word in the Word Bank. Then read the sentence beside it.

biology	The study of **biology** is more than just watching animals.
poetic	She talks in a **poetic** and rhythmic way.
fortunate	Fred was **fortunate** to get the high-paying job.
heroism	Paula showed great **heroism** when she saved the boy.
geology	**Geology** is the study of the earth's structure and history.
kindness	I thanked him for his **kindness** toward the sick.
desperate	The team was **desperate** for a goalie, so they chose me.
historic	The **historic** area was full of houses built at the turn of the century.
loneliness	His **loneliness** was made worse by his friend's absence.
capitalism	We learned how money changes hands in **capitalism**.

Sort: Write each word from the Word Bank under its suffix.

logy	ic	ate	ism	ness
1. _____	3. _____	5. _____	7. _____	9. _____
2. _____	4. _____	6. _____	8. _____	10. _____

Complete: Write a suffix in each blank to spell a word that fits the definition.

11. histor____   *relating to history*

12. kind_____   *quality of being kind*

13. bio_____   *the science of life*

14. capital_____   *system based on capital*

15. fortun_____   *characterized by good fortune*

16. loneli_____   *quality of being lonely*

17. hero_____   *the qualities of a hero*

18. geo_____   *the science of the earth*

19. desper_____   *characterized by despair*

20. poet____   *having the quality of poetry*

Solve: **Write a word from the Word Bank to solve each riddle.**

TECH TIP

21. I'm all over an empty town;
I'm what you feel when no one's around. _____

22. I exist in countries where profits are made;
I'm based on private property and free trade. _____

23. I'm the kind of occurrence you hope for when stuck;
I'm the type of thing brought about by good luck. _____

24. My kind of language has both rhythm and rhyme;
Writers use my words when they have the time. _____

25. Mine is the study of animal features;
I'm the study of life and all living creatures. _____

26. The brave use me to conquer the villain;
The good guys in movies show me again and again. _____

Does your word processing program have a thesaurus? Do you know how to use it? Next time you're having trouble thinking of the right word to use in your writing, highlight the word you want to replace and go to the thesaurus. It can give you some good choices!

Choose: **Write a word from the box to complete each sentence.**

geology	kindness	desperate	historic

27. The rocks found in the cave were clues to the area's _____.

28. Many people enjoy visiting the _____ battlefield.

29. The ship was sinking fast, and the crew was _____.

30. Hannah showed great _____ when she nursed the sick bird.

Proofread: **Read each sentence. Draw a line through the misspelled word. Write the correct spelling on the line.**

31. He had the kindniss to comfort me
during my period of loneliness. _____

32. Someone should write a poetic story
about the heroizm of his act. _____

33. I was desperite for a friend until I was
fortunate enough to meet you. _____

Write: **Write a sentence to answer each question.**

34. What is one act of heroism that you have witnessed?

_____

35. What is a good way to get rid of feelings of loneliness?

_____

LESSON 38   Words with *augh* or *ough*

KNOW

- The letters **augh** and **ough** have different sounds in different words.

- The letters **augh** can stand for the /ô/ sound, as in the word **daughter**, or the /ăf/ sound, as in the word **laugh**.

- The letters **ough** can stand for the long **o** sound, as in the word **though**; the long **oo** sound, as in the word **through**; the /aw/ sound, as in the word **sought**; or the /ŭf/ sound, as in the word **rough**.

Word Bank

Read each word in the Word Bank. Then read the sentence beside it.

tough	The hike was **tough**, but we arrived at camp before dark.
although	**Although** Areej smiled, she was still upset.
caught	Jack **caught** the ball on one hop and threw it to first base.
dough	The cook mixed the **dough** for the cookies.
bought	Nuria **bought** tickets for the play.
slough	A **slough** of muddy water formed behind the beaver dam.
taught	Marcus **taught** the class about the rainy season in India.
laughter	After she finished telling the joke, the classroom filled with **laughter**.
fought	Ben and Felicia **fought** over who would sit in the comfy chair.
ought	You **ought** to wear a raincoat outside today.

Sort: Write each bold word from the box under its rhyme.

rhymes with **thought**	rhymes with **know**	rhymes with **stuff**
1. _____	6. _____	9. _____
2. _____	7. _____	rhymes with **after**
3. _____	rhymes with **too**	10. _____
4. _____	8. _____	
5. _____		

Complete: Write **augh** or **ough** in each blank to spell a word that fits the sentence.

11. Andres t_____t his sister how to ride a horse.

12. I always hear his l_____ter when he watches that show.

13. The boxers f_____t for ten rounds.

14. Alth_____ we were late, we c_____t the train.

15. We needed yeast to make the d_____ rise.

Match: Draw a line from each word to its meaning.

16. laughter   • a muddy hole or pond

17. tough   • purchased

18. dough   • seized or grabbed

19. bought   • giggling

20. caught   • difficult

21. slough   • a thick mixture used in baking

SPELLING BUILDER

Words that are spelled the same but have different meanings are homographs. **Slough** is a homograph. It rhymes with **blue** and means "a muddy body of water." **Slough** can also rhyme with **rough** and mean "to shed or come off."

Choose: Write a word from the box to complete each sentence.

although	taught	ought	fought

22. Ike _____ in the war and came home a hero.

23. _____ Tram liked the ring, he couldn't buy it.

24. You _____ to meet the new coach.

25. Vic _____ a painting class last week.

Proofread: Read each sentence. Draw a line through the misspelled word. Write the correct spelling on the line.

26. Mark fought against his fears and baught a ticket for the roller coaster. _____

27. Chandra tought the class about straits and sloughs. _____

28. Although the sun was in his eyes, Kip cought the ball. _____

29. We had a tuff time mixing the dough. _____

30. The children's laughter aught to made him feel better. _____

Write: Write a sentence to answer each question.

31. What is one thing you have taught someone else to do?

_____

32. What is one tough task you have completed this year?

_____

KNOW

- Every syllable has a vowel sound. You can count the syllables in a word by listening to the number of vowel sounds.

- Breaking words into syllables can help you spell them.

- If you have trouble breaking a word into syllables, you can use the dictionary to find where the word splits.

VOCABULARY BUILDER

Some names of creatures can be made into adjectives by adding a suffix. For example, the suffix **ian** can be added to **reptile** to make the adjective **reptilian**, meaning "like a reptile." The suffix **ous** can be added to **carnivore** to make the adjective **carnivorous**, meaning "meat-eating."

Word Bank

Read each word in the Word Bank. Then read the sentence beside it.

insect	A bee is a very busy **insect**.
amphibian	An **amphibian** is at home on land and in water.
reptile	A snake is a type of **reptile** that has no legs.
mammal	A whale is a **mammal** that lives in the sea.
marsupial	A red kangaroo is a large **marsupial** native to Australia.
lizard	The scaly **lizard** warmed itself on a sunny rock.
carnivore	A **carnivore** eats meat.
herbivore	The **herbivore** enjoyed a meal of tender leaves.
mollusk	An oyster is a hard-shelled **mollusk** that can produce a shiny pearl.
worm	The **worm** wriggled in the pile of dirt.

Sort: Write each word from the Word Bank in the correct place.

one syllable	two syllables	three syllables	four syllables
1. _____	2. _____	7. _____	9. _____
	3. _____	8. _____	10. _____
	4. _____		
	5. _____		
	6. _____		

Complete: Write the missing syllable to spell a word that fits the sentence.

11. A female mam_____ produces milk to feed her young.

12. A marsu_____al protects its young in a pouch outside the body.

13. A _____lusk has a soft body, often with a hard outer shell.

14. A cow is an herbi_____ that eats mostly grass.

15. A liz_____ has scales, a tail, and usually four legs.

16. A _____tile has a backbone, scales, and lungs for breathing air.

Label: Write the type of animal for each picture on the right. Use the Word Bank. There is more than one answer for some pictures.

17. _____

20. _____

18. _____

21. _____

19. _____

22. _____

Choose: Write a word from the box to complete each sentence.

| reptile | marsupial | carnivore | herbivore |

23. A lion is a fierce _____.

24. A crocodile is a large, scaly _____.

25. A rabbit is an _____ with long ears and soft fur.

26. A wombat is a _____ that looks like a small bear.

Proofread: Read each sentence. Draw a line through the misspelled word. Write the correct spelling on the line.

27. An amfibian and a reptile are both cold-blooded creatures. _____

28. A deer is a mammal and an herbivor. _____

29. Many inseckts fly, but all worms crawl. _____

30. A kangaroo is a marsoopial but not a carnivore. _____

31. Lizards generally stay on land, while molusks stay in or beside the sea. _____

Write: Write a sentence to answer each question.

32. Which type of insect do you dislike the most?

_____

33. Which type of mammal would you like to see in the wild?

_____

17.

18.

19.

20.

21.

22.

LESSON 40   Adverbs for Accurate Descriptions

■ An **adverb** can make a sentence more descriptive. It can be used to tell about a verb, an adjective, or another adverb.

■ An adverb can tell **when, where,** or **how.** It can give information about time, place, manner, or degree.

Word Bank

Read each word in the Word Bank. Then read the sentence beside it.

constantly	Angie **constantly** seeks the advice of her older sister Karen.
swiftly	The rabbit ran **swiftly** into the forest.
silently	David and I walked **silently** along the beach.
angrily	Uta stormed off **angrily** after arguing with Beth.
joyfully	The choir sang **joyfully**.
fiercely	A lioness will **fiercely** protect her cubs.
scarcely	I had **scarcely** reached home when it began to rain.
casually	Mica was dressed more **casually** than the other party guests.
sullenly	The kids went **sullenly** to bed at 8:30.
proudly	Dad **proudly** showed us the large fish he had caught.

Sort: Write each adverb from the Word Bank next to the adjective it is related to.

1. scarce _____

2. angry _____

3. joyful _____

4. swift _____

5. casual _____

6. silent _____

7. proud _____

8. constant _____

9. fierce _____

10. sullen _____

Complete: Write the missing letters in each blank to spell a word that fits the sentence.

11. The birds flew sw_____ly to the treetops.

12. Our lunch break is so short, we scar_____ly have time to eat.

13. The kids joy_____ly ran home after practice.

14. Taylor walked cas_____lly past the crime scene.

15. Melissa is const_____tly worried about something.

102   Chapter 5

Circle: Circle the word that means almost the same as the bold word.

16. **constantly**   secretly   regularly   kindly

17. **swiftly**   powerfully   calmly   quickly

18. **silently**   noiselessly   modestly   politely

19. **joyfully**   actively   happily   loudly

20. **scarcely**   hardly   gently   cleverly

WRITING TIP

Adding some adverbs to your writing can make it more interesting and lively. Use adverbs wisely; be careful not to use too many adverbs. Too many adverbs can make your writing sound unnatural and forced.

Choose: Write a word from the box to complete each sentence.

| angrily | fiercely | casually | sullenly | proudly |

21. My sister _____ showed us the medal she had just won.

22. We like to dress _____ when we go out to dinner.

23. Jake _____ slammed the car door.

24. Not wanting to admit she was wrong, Evelyn _____ apologized to her brother.

25. Gina _____ guards her diary, locking it in a drawer every day.

Proofread: Read each sentence. Draw a line through the misspelled word. Write the correct spelling on the line.

26. The villain glared angryly as the hero and his sweetheart joyfully embraced. _____

27. Jane fiercly defended the soccer goal, while her mother watched proudly. _____

28. Lori greeted us casuelly and then went swiftly to work. _____

29. The princess walked sulenly and silently to her chamber. _____

Write: Write a sentence to answer each question.

30. What is one chore that you are able to do swiftly?

_____

31. What is an activity that you do joyfully?

_____

Part A

Complete: For each set, write a word from the list to complete each sentence.

caution   **A**
sensation
veteran
curtain

1. I felt a strange _____ when I flew in a glider.
2. There will be less light in the room if you close the _____.
3. Lynn is one of our _____ employees.
4. Use _____ when walking down the icy street!

career   **B**
ceramic
submerge
interrupt

5. She made several fine _____ objects in pottery class.
6. The whale will _____ for about twenty minutes.
7. Terry is starting a new _____ as a writer.
8. Please do not _____ me while I'm speaking!

fortunate   **C**
loneliness
although
laughter

9. I don't camp by myself because I can't stand _____.
10. You were _____ not to be hurt when you fell.
11. The comedian enjoyed hearing _____ from the crowd.
12. _____ she felt tired, Karen still went to the party.

amphibian   **D**
carnivore
angrily
scarcely

13. Molly _____ denied taking Darren's pen.
14. Fred _____ had time to put on his shoes.
15. An _____ is born in water.
16. The lion is a _____ that feeds mostly on herbivores.

Sort: For each set, write the words from the list in the correct place.

ceramic   **E**
sensation
veteran
although

	ends in /ən/ spelled **an**		rhymes with **know**
17. _____		19.	_____
	/ə/ spelled **e** in the first syllable		ending pronounced /shən/
18. _____		20.	_____

loneliness   **F**
submerge
interrupt
fortunate

	words with prefixes		words with suffixes
21. _____		23.	_____
22. _____		24.	_____

Complete: Write the missing letter or letters to spell each word. Look back at the lists on page 104 if you need help.

25. scarce__ __

26. cau__ __ __ __

27. am__ __ __bian

28. ve__ __ran

29. __ __though

30. for__ __nate

31. __ __ramic

32. subm__ __ge

33. __ __ __ __ __rupt

34. car__ __ __

35. lone__ __ness

36. l__ __ __ __ter

37. carni__ __ __ __

38. cur__ __ __ __

39. angr__ly

40. sen__ __tion

Proofread: Read each sentence. Draw a line through the misspelled word. Write the correct spelling on the line.

41. I could scarsely believe it when I heard laughter coming from the room. _____

42. The tiny amfibian sought to submerge itself in the pond. _____

43. The tired deer was fortunate not to be seen by a hungry carnevore. _____

44. Zac angrily started to interupt the store manager. _____

45. Although her carear was going well, Tina wanted to find a new job. _____

46. Please handle that seramic jar with caution! _____

47. The veteren lighthouse operator was familiar with loneliness. _____

48. Lisa felt a strange sensashion as she pulled back the curtain. _____

Write: Write a sentence to answer each question.

49. In what activity or job do you consider yourself a veteran?

_____

_____

50. About what do you feel most fortunate?

_____

_____

Part B

Complete: For each set, write a word from the list to complete each sentence.

A

promotion

persuasion

urban

reason

1. Can you give me a _____ why you didn't do your homework?
2. I like living in an _____ area with many places to go.
3. Amy used her powers of _____ to convince her dad to take her to the circus.
4. Ramon was hoping for a _____ at work.

B

itemize

oblige

coordinate

antibody

5. I'm sorry, but I can't _____ your request for a raise.
6. The blood produces an _____ to fight the toxin.
7. The leader must _____ everyone's efforts.
8. The clerk will _____ the charges on the bill.

C

desperate

capitalism

ought

slough

9. The frog jumped into the muddy _____ .
10. The river rose higher, and the situation became _____ .
11. You _____ to wear sunscreen at the beach.
12. Private property is a key element of _____ .

D

marsupial

mollusk

fiercely

sullenly

13. After being scolded, Mark stared _____ at the wall.
14. A kangaroo is one type of _____ .
15. The mother bear _____ protected her cubs.
16. An octopus is a _____ with no outer shell.

Match: Draw a line from each word to its meaning.

E

17. sullenly   • an effort to convince someone
18. persuasion   • a muddy body of water
19. slough   • mammal with a pouch to hold its young
20. marsupial   • in a way that is angry and brooding

F

21. desperate   • relating to a city
22. urban   • almost without hope
23. itemize   • to make people work together
24. coordinate   • to list item by item

Solve: Use the words from the lists on page 106 to fill in the puzzle.

Across
27. U.S. economic system
30. intensely
31. cause; motive
32. to put in a list
34. to satisfy or serve
36. should think in a certain way
37. clam, snail, or octopus
38. an advancement at work
39. waterway in a swamp
40. city-like

Down
25. very bad; almost hopeless
26. virus-fighter in the blood
28. to organize in a common action
29. kangaroo, opossum, or wombat
33. the power to get someone to act
35. in a moody, angry way

Proofread: Read each sentence. Draw a line through the misspelled word. Write the correct spelling on the line.

41. My boss will oblige my request for a promosion. _____

42. You ought to use your powers of persuasion more often. _____

43. Growing up in an urben area, I never saw a slough. _____

44. Give me a reason why we should itumize these costs. _____

45. The scientist was desparate to find the correct antibody. _____

46. The leader argued fiersely in support of capitalism. _____

47. Greta sullenly put the mollisk back into the tidepool. _____

48. A biologist will coordenate the workers who will study marsupials in the wild. _____

Write: Write a sentence to answer each question.

49. When did you coordinate people in order to get something done?

_____

50. When have you successfully used persuasion?

_____

CHAPTER 6

LESSON 41   Related Word Forms

KNOW

■ Some words have several related forms. For example, the words **editor, edition,** and **editorial** are related forms of the word **edit.**

■ Knowing how to spell a word can help you spell its related forms correctly.

Word Bank

Read each word in the Word Bank. Then read the sentence beside it.

produce	Each group must **produce** a report that describes its project.
producer	The company is a **producer** of toys and games.
production	We saw a stunning **production** of the opera *Carmen*.
productive	Our meeting with Professor Carnoy was very **productive**.
productively	Josh works most **productively** early in the morning.
collide	I just saw two people **collide** in the hallway.
collision	Carol witnessed a minor **collision** on the freeway.
receive	Did you **receive** an invitation in the mail?
receipt	The shopkeeper gave me a **receipt** for my purchase.
reception	We went to Joanna's wedding **reception**.

Sort: **Write each word from the Word Bank under the related word form.**

colliding	receptive	product
1. _____	3. _____	6. _____
2. _____	4. _____	7. _____
	5. _____	8. _____
		9. _____
		10. _____

Complete: **Write the missing letters in each blank to spell a word that fits the sentence.**

11. What happens when two particles coll_____?

12. Jill had a produc_____ day at work.

13. Students will rec_____ve their report cards in two weeks.

14. Who was the pro_____cer of that comedy show?

15. Did you attend the recep_____ at Carla's house?

Match: Draw a line from each word to its meaning.

16. producer   • to make or create

17. reception   • to get or obtain

18. collide   • one who makes or creates something

19. produce   • a social function or party

20. receive   • to bump into each other

READING TIP

Sometimes the same letter is pronounced differently in two related words. For example, the **c** in **produce** stands for the /s/ sound, while in **productive** it stands for the /k/ sound.

Choose: Write a word from the box to complete each sentence.

production	productive	productively	collision	receipt

21. The team of scientists worked _____ through the night.

22. Sam swerved to avoid a _____.

23. Sean says he is more _____ in the morning.

24. I asked the store clerk for a _____.

25. The factory workers were praised for the increase in _____.

Proofread: Read each sentence. Draw a line through the misspelled word. Write the correct spelling on the line.

26. Li hopes to produce a new machine that will cause atoms to colide. _____

27. The produser of the play viewed the final production. _____

28. On a productive day, Glen can produse three paintings. _____

29. Make sure that all the guests receive a warm recepcion. _____

30. You must produce your receit in order to return these items. _____

31. The crew worked produtcively to clean up after the collision. _____

Write: Write a sentence to answer each question.

32. At what time of day are you most productive?

_____

33. Why is it important to get a receipt when you buy something?

_____

LESSON 42   Words with Greek or Latin Roots

KNOW

■ Many words in English originally came from Greek or Latin words. Knowing Greek and Latin roots can help you figure out the meanings of English words related to them.

Some Greek root words:
• kuklos means "circle"
• metron means "measure"
• optos means "seen"
• pathos means "feeling"
• skopein means "to see"
• tele means "far off"
• thermos means "warm, hot"

Some Latin root words:
• credere means "to believe"
• dicere means "to say"
• rumpere means "to break"
• videre means "to see"
• volvere means "to roll"

Word Bank

Read each word in the Word Bank. Then read the sentence beside it.

bicycle	Robin rode his **bicycle** to school.
credit	My father gave me **credit** for doing my chores without complaining.
erupt	Is that volcano going to **erupt**?
optical	The doctor used **optical** instruments to test my vision.
video	My brother rented a movie at the **video** store.
thermometer	The **thermometer** showed that I had a fever.
predict	Naomi tried to **predict** who would win the race.
telescope	Neil put his eye to the **telescope** and saw stars.
revolve	Earth is one of nine planets that **revolve** around our sun.
sympathy	Cleo had **sympathy** for the girl who forgot her lunch.

Sort: Compare the Greek and Latin roots with the words in the Word Bank. Then write each word from the Word Bank on the correct line.

Words with Greek Roots   Words with Latin Roots

1. _____   3. _____   6. _____   9. _____

2. _____   4. _____   7. _____   10. _____

5. _____   8. _____

Complete: Write the Greek or Latin word and its meaning in the correct blanks.

11. The word **bicycle** comes from the Greek word _____, meaning "_____."

12. The word **sympathy** comes from the Greek word _____, meaning "_____."

13. The word **video** comes from the Latin word _____, meaning "_____."

14. The word **erupt** comes from the Latin word _____, meaning "_____."

15. The word **revolve** comes from the Latin word _____, meaning "_____."

Match: Draw a line from each word to its meaning.

16. optical • something that measures cold and heat

17. predict • to explode or release

18. erupt • having to do with sight

19. thermometer • having to do with television

20. revolve • to turn around a central point

21. video • to tell about what will or might happen

Choose: Write a word from the box to complete each sentence.

telescope	sympathy	credit	bicycle

22. The assistant coach took _____ for helping the team win the game.

23. Pauline did not want to ride her _____ to the store.

24. That scientist was studying the planets with a _____.

25. The teacher had _____ for the student who forgot his lines in the play.

Proofread: Read each sentence. Draw a line through the misspelled word. Write the correct spelling on the line.

26. I tried to pridict what the thermometer would read. _____

27. We felt sympathy for the boy who had lost his bicicle. _____

28. A telescope is an optikal instrument. _____

29. Lana got full credit for directing the wonderful vidio. _____

30. How do you make a top reevolve? _____

31. The volcano might irupt any day now. _____

Write: Write a sentence to answer each question.

32. What is your favorite video of all time?

_____

33. What would you look at first if you had a telescope?

_____

LESSON 43   Final -*able*, -*ible*

KNOW

■ A suffix is a word part that can be added to the end of a word. It changes the meaning of the word. The suffixes **able** and **ible** mean "likely or able to." They are both pronounced /əbəl/, as in the words **horrible** and **durable**.

■ When the suffix **able** is added to words ending with **c** or **g** and silent **e**, that final **e** is kept:

change + able = changeable.

■ When the suffix **able** is added to other words ending in silent **e**, that final **e** is usually dropped:

use + able = usable.

Word Bank

Read each word in the Word Bank. Then read the sentence beside it.

possible	Alexis picked some **possible** dates for his party.
portable	My brother brings his **portable** phone everywhere.
lovable	Dave's puppy was cute and **lovable**.
terrible	The **terrible** fire ruined the forest.
visible	The fish were **visible** in the clear water.
noticeable	The improvement in her mood was **noticeable**.
capable	I am quite **capable** of feeding the cats this week!
edible	Are those mushrooms **edible**?
likeable	The **likeable** coach never raised his voice with the team.
usable	Although the bicycle is old, it's still **usable**.

Sort: Write each word from the Word Bank on the correct line.

words with **able**   words with **ible**

1. _____   7. _____

2. _____   8. _____

3. _____   9. _____

4. _____   10. _____

5. _____

6. _____

Complete: Write **able** or **ible** in each blank to spell a word that fits the sentence.

11. Winning the game was poss_____.

12. The kitten was soft and lov_____.

13. The cast was vis_____ at the back of the stage.

14. Laura is cap_____ of hiking.

15. The terr_____ storm caused waves to splash over the boat.

16. Those flowers are ed_____

17. The radio was port_____ so we took it to the beach with us.

18. Marnie is a like_____ person.

19. The change in Sui's height was notice_____.

20. The scuffed ball wasn't us_____.

Solve: Write a word from the Word Bank to solve each riddle.

21. I can often be a tasty treat;
    But really I am anything you can eat. _____

22. You move me from here to there;
    You can take me anywhere. _____

23. I'm a flower, a book, a train, a tree;
    I'm everything that you can see. _____

24. I'm awful, scary, mean, and bad;
    I'm things that make you mad or sad. _____

25. I may not be lovable, but I'm your friend;
    You have good feelings about me in the end. _____

Choose: Write a word from the box to complete each sentence.

capable	lovable	usable	noticeable	possible

26. It is _____ to climb that cliff, but it is safer to follow the trail.

27. That koala looks _____, but it will scratch you if you try to hug it.

28. After Kyle cut the lawn, the difference was _____.

29. That runner is _____ of setting a record.

30. That rake is missing some teeth, but it is _____.

Proofread: Read each sentence. Draw a line through the misspelled word. Write the correct spelling on the line.

31. Is it possible that those leaves are edable? _____

32. She is capable of carrying the portible table. _____

33. The few gray hairs visable on his head are
    very noticeable in direct sunlight. _____

Write: Write a sentence to answer each question.

34. What is the most noticeable feature of your school?

    _____

35. What makes you a likeable person?

    _____

KNOW

- The letters **k, g, b, n,** and **s** appear as silent letters in certain words.

- The letter **k** is often silent when it comes before the letter **n**, as in the word **knit**.

- The letter **g** is often silent when it comes before the letter **n**, as in the word **resign**.

- The letter **b** is often silent when it comes after the letter **m**, as in the word **crumb**.

- The letter **n** is often silent when it comes after the letter **m**, as in the word **solemn**.

- The letter **s** is often silent when it comes after the letter **i** and before the letter **l**, as in the word **isle**.

Word Bank

Read each word in the Word Bank. Then read the sentence beside it.

knock	Don't forget to **knock** on the door before entering.
design	Parul presented her mural **design** to the class.
limb	The weight of the children caused the tree **limb** to snap.
bombing	The girls are **bombing** the boys' camp with water balloons.
island	We studied the wild birds and exotic flowers on the **island**.
knowledge	Gretchen's **knowledge** of art history is impressive.
column	The large **column** helps to support the roof of the building.
align	The teacher asked his students to **align** the tables.
thumb	Sarah cleaned and bandaged the cut on her **thumb**.
kneel	The police officer had to **kneel** down to speak to the little girl.

Sort and Circle: **Write each word from the Word Bank under its description. Then circle the silent letter in each word.**

silent k	silent g	silent b	silent n
1. _____	4. _____	6. _____	9. _____
2. _____	5. _____	7. _____	silent s
3. _____		8. _____	10. _____

Complete: **Write the missing letters in each blank to spell a word that fits the sentence.**

11. We had a relaxing weekend on the _____land.

12. The gardener sawed off the rotting tree li_____.

13. Did you see the desi_____ for the new auditorium?

14. Kim sprained her thu_____ while trying to do a cartwheel.

15. The company wants to hire someone with _____ledge about computers.

Circle: Circle the word that is closest in meaning to the bold word.

16. **knock**   ring   open   tap

17. **design**   brush   sketch   chair

18. **bombing**   attacking   daring   alarming

19. **knowledge**   vision   computer   awareness

20. **column**   roof   pillar   wall

21. **align**   straighten   confuse   crack

TECH TIP

Use the spell checker on your computer if you are not sure whether a word contains a silent letter.

Solve: Write a word from the box to solve each riddle.

limb	island	thumb	kneel

22. Bending a knee helps you do this. _____

23. I am always surrounded by water. _____

24. I can be used to describe an arm, wing, or branch. _____

25. You point me upward when everything is okay. _____

Proofread: Read each sentence. Draw a line through the misspelled word. Write the correct spelling on the line.

26. Our guide shared his knowlege of the island with us. _____

27. Which lim must you bend in order to kneel? _____

28. We should aline the chairs so that we don't knock into them. _____

29. Jesse trimmed the nail on his left thum. _____

30. Did Joseph desing that new museum on the island? _____

31. Bombing in World War II caused damage to a columb in the cathedral. _____

Write: Write a sentence to answer each question.

32. About what subject do you have a lot of knowledge?

_____

33. What would you bring with you on a trip to a tropical island?

_____

LESSON 45   *ie* and *ei* Words

- Words that contain the **ie** or **ei** vowel combination usually follow this rule: "Use i before e except after c, and in words with the long **a** sound, as in **weigh**."

- There are exceptions to this rule.

Word Bank

Read each word in the Word Bank. Then read the sentence beside it.

field	We drove by a **field** of sunflowers.
height	What is the **height** of the Eiffel Tower?
their	David and Liz are hosting a party at **their** house.
friend	My **friend** Katia and I are going to a concert.
piece	Did you get a **piece** of cake?
neighbor	Paola's **neighbor** baked cookies for her.
view	The **view** of the canyon is spectacular!
weigh	How much does the baby **weigh**?
chief	Jodie is the **chief** nurse at the hospital.
veil	Sophie helped the bride put on her wedding **veil**.

Sort: **Write each word from the Word Bank under its description.**

words with **ie**   words with **ei**

1. _____   6. _____

2. _____   7. _____

3. _____   8. _____

4. _____   9. _____

5. _____   10. _____

Complete: **Write ie or ei in each blank to spell a word that fits the sentence.**

11. This p_____ce of cake is bigger than that one.

12. Misha greeted her n_____ghbor Bill at the block party.

13. Toby invited a fr_____nd to the harvest festival.

14. Joseph tends the f_____ld behind his grandmother's cottage.

15. How much does this suitcase w_____gh?

Solve: Write a word from the Word Bank to solve each riddle. Think about the shape of each word.

16. ☐☐☐☐☐   I am a leader. I am the person in charge.

17. ☐☐☐☐☐☐☐   I live next door.

18. ☐☐☐☐☐   I am someone you trust.

19. ☐☐☐☐☐   I describe how tall you are.

20. ☐☐☐☐☐   I am one part of something.

Choose: Write a word from the box to complete each sentence.

field	their	view	weigh	veil

21. James and Ben ordered _____ favorite pasta.

22. Jessica's little sister likes to play with her mother's wedding _____.

23. My cousin is planting soybeans in that _____.

24. We had to crowd around the table to _____ the demonstration.

25. The zookeeper had to _____ the baby hippo.

WRITING TIP

When you proofread your work, check to make sure you have used the correct words in these homophone sets:
their   there   they're
piece   peace
weigh   way
veil   vale

Proofread: Read each sentence. Draw a line through the misspelled word. Write the correct spelling on the line.

26. The judge will wiegh each pumpkin and then measure its height and circumference. _____

27. My friend and I walked briskly across the feild. _____

28. The daughter of the chief wore a hat with a viel to the ceremony. _____

29. I brought a peice of pie to my grandfather. _____

Write: Write a sentence to answer each question.

30. From where can you get the best view of your city or town?

_____

31. How can you tell if someone is a true friend?

_____

LESSON 46   Silent Letters *t, w, h, p, l*

KNOW

- Some words have unusual spellings in which certain consonants are silent.

- The letter **t** is usually silent in words ending in **stle**, such as **rustle**.

- The letter **w** is usually silent when followed by the letter **r**, as in **wrap**.

- The letter **h** is usually silent when it follows the letter **g** at the beginning of a word, as in **ghost**.

- The letter **p** is sometimes silent when followed by the letter **b**, as in **raspberry**.

- The letter **l** is sometimes silent when followed by the letter **m**, as in **calm**.

Word Bank

Read each word in the Word Bank. Then read the sentence beside it.

hustle	I woke up late and had to **hustle** to get to school on time.
wrong	Your ideas are correct, but your answer is **wrong**.
honor	The committee awarded the **honor** to Jamila.
almond	Wally's favorite nut is the **almond**.
cupboard	The **cupboard** is full of cups and dishes.
wreath	Randy made a **wreath** of flowers and hung it above the fireplace.
salmon	The **salmon** begins and ends its life cycle in fresh water.
psychology	Max studied **psychology** because he was interested in the human mind.
ghastly	He will be severely punished for his **ghastly** crime.
castle	The princess slept in the tallest tower of the **castle**.

Sort: Write each word from the Word Bank under its description.

silent t	silent h	silent l
1. _____	5. _____	9. _____
2. _____	6. _____	10. _____

silent w	silent p
3. _____	7. _____
4. _____	8. _____

Complete: Write the missing letter in each blank to spell a word that fits the sentence.

11. Use this sponge to wipe out that cu_____board.

12. What is making that g_____astly screeching noise?

13. It is an _____onor to be introduced to an ambassador.

14. That pine _____reath makes the whole apartment smell nice!

15. My home is my cas_____le.

Match: Draw a line from each word to its synonym.

16. wrong • terrible

17. castle • rush

18. ghastly • cabinet

19. honor • incorrect

20. cupboard • fortress

21. hustle • tribute

Choose: Write a word from the box to complete each sentence.

almond	wreath	salmon	psychology

22. The packet of nuts had five peanuts, three cashews, and one _____.

23. Many who study _____ become fascinated by the abilities of the human mind.

24. You should take down that _____ because its flowers are withering.

25. The _____ swam upstream, back to its birthplace.

Proofread: Read each sentence. Draw a line through the misspelled word. Write the correct spelling on the line.

26. I may have dropped an amond behind the cupboard. _____

27. Aren't those samon swimming in the wrong direction? _____

28. The scientist was awarded the honor for her work in sychology. _____

29. That reath looks pretty, but the pink and black cake looks ghastly! _____

30. We had to hustle to get to the casle on time. _____

Write: Write a sentence to answer each question.

31. What is one honor you would like to receive?

_____

32. Would you like to live in a castle? Why or why not?

_____

VOCABULARY BUILDER

The root **psych** means "relating to the mind." It comes from the Greek word **psukhe**, meaning "life" or "spirit." The letter **p** is always silent in words beginning with **psych**. Some words with this root are **psychic**, **psychosis**, **psychology**, and **psychologist**.

LESSON 47   Words About Characters

KNOW

- Almost every activity has its own set of specific words for objects and actions related to it.

- Learning words that have to do with characters and their actions in stories, novels, or plays can help you talk and write about literature.

Word Bank

Read each word in the Word Bank. Then read the sentence beside it.

character	The main **character** in the story is charming and funny.
hero	In my favorite comic book, the **hero** performs daring feats.
villain	A **villain** is usually devising some kind of terrible plot.
conflict	The story's main **conflict** is between the Sharks and the Jets.
trait	Her best **trait** is her honesty.
motive	What is the **motive** behind his choice to be a detective?
monologue	A **monologue** is when one person makes a long speech.
dialogue	The **dialogue** between Tony and Maria was quick and witty.
gesture	As he spoke, he waved his arms in a dramatic **gesture**.
accent	Adra speaks with a British **accent**.

Sort: Write each word from the Word Bank under the correct description.

Something that a person in a story can be . . .	Something that a person in a story can have . . .	Something that a person in a story can say or do . . .
1. _____	4. _____	8. _____
2. _____	5. _____	9. _____
3. _____	6. _____	10. _____
	7. _____	

Complete: Write the missing syllable in each blank to spell a word that fits the sentence.

11. The _____lain sneered.

12. Cara performed the mono_____ slowly and clearly.

13. His _____cent told me that he was from France.

14. That charac_____ starts a band.

15. The _____ro of the story is noble and brave.

16. Frank likes to ges_____ with his hands while he speaks.

17. What was Tom's _____tive for keeping the secret for so long?

Match: Draw a line from each word to its meaning.

18. motive   • a fictional person in book, movie, or play

19. gesture   • a wicked character

20. dialogue   • a disagreement; tension

21. character   • a reason why someone does something

22. conflict   • a conversation between two or more people

23. villain   • a body movement made to help express an idea

SPELLING BUILDER

Several words in this lesson have unusual spellings that you should memorize. **Ch** stands for the /k/ sound in **character**, **ai** stands for the schwa or /ə/ in **villain**, and **ue** is silent in both **monologue** and **dialogue**.

Choose: Write a word from the box to complete each sentence.

hero	trait	monologue	accent

24. Jay left out a few lines when he spoke the _____.

25. The _____ of the story saved a child's life.

26. Can you speak those lines without a French _____?

27. His worst _____ is that he can be selfish.

Proofread: Read each sentence. Draw a line through the misspelled word. Write the correct spelling on the line.

28. The hero and the villin have been enemies for years. _____

29. The conflict is between the main caracter and her brother. _____

30. What is the motive behind the jesture she made?_____

31. The actor performed the monologe with a Spanish accent._____

32. The actor's most visible trate is his confidence. _____

33. The dialague in this play is not realistic. _____

Write: Write a sentence to answer each question.

34. Who is your favorite character in a book you've read recently?

_____

35. What is one of your personal traits that you are proud of?

_____

LESSON 48   Words About Events

- Learning words that have to do with events in stories, novels, or plays can help you talk and write about literature.

- Remember what you know about syllables. Breaking long words into syllables can help you read and spell them.

Word Bank

Read each word in the Word Bank. Then read the sentence beside it.

event	The most important **event** of the school year is graduation.
suspense	**Suspense** in the mystery keeps me guessing what's next.
irony	The play's **irony** is that the audience knows the truth, but the characters don't.
narrator	A **narrator** tells the story in his or her own voice.
sequence	The **sequence** of events in this story is hard to follow.
foreshadow	Writers sometimes **foreshadow** events before they happen.
flashback	The book contained a vivid **flashback** to a character's past.
climax	Lex's discovery of a secret was the **climax** of the story.
resolution	The **resolution** of the story began after the fight had ended.
conclusion	At the **conclusion** of the book, everyone became friends.

Sort: Write each word from the Word Bank under the correct term.

two syllables		three syllables	four syllables
1. _____	4. _____	6. _____	10. _____
2. _____	5. _____	7. _____	
3. _____		8. _____	
		9. _____	

Complete: Write the missing letters in each blank to spell a word that fits the sentence.

11. The narra_____ told the story in an enjoyable way.

12. The book had a strong _____clusion after a weak middle.

13. Detective novels are often dark and filled with _____pense.

14. The character had a flash_____ to the first time she saw snow.

15. What is the first important e_____ that happens in the play?

16. The _____max of the story was when the son finally came home.

17. A clear resolu_____ is needed to make sense of this confusing story.

Match: Draw a line from each word to its meaning.

18. climax   • someone who tells a story

19. flashback   • something that takes place

20. narrator   • last part of something

21. event   • order of events

22. conclusion   • the retelling of an episode that took place in the past

23. sequence   • the most dramatic point in a sequence of events

Use the words from this lesson and the previous one when you write about works of literature. You can use the precise terms in these lessons to help you describe the various elements in a story.

Choose: Write a word from the box to complete each sentence.

| suspense | irony | foreshadow | resolution |

24. The writer uses clues to _____ the ending of the story.

25. _____ happens when readers know something that characters don't.

26. The book had a satisfying _____ and a happy ending.

27. The _____ in the spy film kept me on the edge of my seat.

Proofread: Read each sentence. Draw a line through the misspelled word. Write the correct spelling on the line.

28. In the play, there was a flashbak to an event from ten years ago. _____

29. The intense suspense led up to a very dramatic climacks. _____

30. When readers know something, the narrater doesn't, that's irony.

_____

31. The sequense of events leading up to the conclusion was confusing._____

32. Did the author forshadow the resolution of the conflict? _____

Write: Write a sentence to answer each question.

33. Do you like to read books with a lot of suspense? Why or why not?

_____

34. What was the most important event in a movie you saw recently?

_____

Part A

Complete: For each set, write a word from the list to complete each sentence.

collision	**A**
receive	
erupt	
sympathy	

1. Scientists predict that the volcano will _____ within ten years.
2. Marcus had _____ for the boy who had lost his homework.
3. You should _____ the letter by Friday.
4. Tammy avoided a _____ with the other skater.

lovable	**B**
noticeable	
design	
limb	

5. The architect used a computer to _____ the building.
6. The huge tree _____ snapped during the storm.
7. The dark stain was very _____ on the tablecloth.
8. Megan's teddy bear is cute and _____.

height	**C**
view	
honor	
wreath	

9. Winning this award is a great _____.
10. Owen hung a _____ to decorate the door.
11. The _____ of that giraffe is more than 17 feet!
12. We had a clear _____ of the game from our seats.

monologue	**D**
dialogue	
sequence	
climax	

13. Stuart gave a short _____ to the class.
14. A timeline shows events in _____.
15. The final battle was the _____ of the story.
16. I enjoyed the _____ between those characters.

Sort: For each set, write the words from the list in the correct place.

design	**E**
view	
height	
limb	

long **i** spelled **eigh**	/m/ spelled **mb**
17. _____	19. _____
/n/ spelled **gn**	long /yoo/ spelled **iew**
18. _____	20. _____

erupt	**F**
lovable	
sympathy	
noticeable	

words with a Greek or Latin root	words with suffixes
21. _____	23. _____
22. _____	24. _____

Complete: Write the missing letter or letters to spell each word. Look back at the lists on page 124 if you need help.

25. colli__ __ __ __

26. sequen__ __

27. dialo__ __ __

28. notic__ __ble

29. s__mpathy

30. lim__

31. __reath

32. clim__ __

33. h__ __ght

34. desi__n

35. __onor

36. lo__ __ __le

37. __ __nologue

38. eru__ __

39. rec__ __ve

40. v__ __w

Proofread: Read each sentence. Draw a line through the misspelled word. Write the correct spelling on the line.

41. I should recieve sympathy for having such bad luck. _____

42. The building's height makes it noticable from a distance. _____

43. The monologe was spoken during a strange sequence of events in the play. _____

44. The eagle must have a great veiw of the valley from its perch on the tree limb. _____

45. The geologists had a nervous dilogue about when the volcano might erupt. _____

46. Cindy was given a floral reath and a lovable doll. _____

47. It would be an honor to desine the statue. _____

48. The collision of the trucks was the climacks of the movie. _____

Write: Write a sentence to answer each question.

49. For whom do you have a lot of sympathy?

_____

_____

50. What is the most amazing view you have ever seen?

_____

_____

Part B

Complete: For each set, write a word from the list to complete each sentence.

A

productive
receipt
credit
optical

1. Manny deserves _____ for building the model.
2. Binoculars and a camera are both _____ instruments.
3. You'll need a _____ to prove that you purchased the items here.
4. June was the most _____ month ever.

B

capable
portable
knowledge
align

5. Is Vernon _____ of finding the museum by himself?
6. A veterinarian must have _____ of many animals.
7. Please _____ the desks in three parallel rows.
8. Let's bring the _____ stove to the campground.

C

neighbor
veil
psychology
ghastly

9. _____ is the scientific study of the mind.
10. The crash resulted in a _____ scene.
11. I asked my _____ to help fix the fence between our yards.
12. The bride wore a beautiful _____ at the wedding.

D

conflict
motive
suspense
irony

13. What was the burglar's _____ for taking my shoe polish?
14. Denny and Mick settled their _____ by talking.
15. The _____ was that the tallest player's last name was "Short."
16. The mystery was packed with _____ and thrills.

Match: Draw a line from each word to its meaning.

E

17. optical
18. receipt
19. neighbor
20. align

• to arrange in a line
• one who lives next door
• relating to sight
• written evidence of payment

F

21. ghastly
22. suspense
23. veil
24. portable

• nervous feeling caused by uncertainty
• cloth worn over the head or face
• easily carried
• horrible or frightening

Solve: Use the words from the lists on page 126 to fill in the puzzle.

Across

27. movable
29. praise; approval for an action
33. nearby resident
34. of or relating to sight
36. something covering the face
37. wisdom
40. feeling resulting from an uncertain situation

Down

25. able to bring forth a good result
26. to line up
28. the science of the mind
30. having ability
31. a reason or cause
32. a sales slip
35. when something is the opposite of what it appears to be
38. terrible; shocking
39. a fight or disagreement

Proofread: Read each sentence. Draw a line through the misspelled word. Write the correct spelling on the line.

41. You should get a reciept for the optical equipment. _____

42. The irony was that *The Great Mystery* featured very little suspence. _____

43. The conflikt had a ghastly result. _____

44. To understand her motive, you must know sychology. _____

45. My naybor let me borrow his portable phone. _____

46. Hire capable employees, and your company will be preductive. _____

47. The bride's veil fell off when she tried to aline the chairs. _____

48. He got credit for having great knoweldge. _____

TEST TIP

Don't just reread the book and study your notes before a test. Make up questions you think the teacher might ask and practice answering them. Better yet, you and a friend can make up questions and then trade question lists.

Write: Write a sentence to answer each question.

49. In what type of activity do you feel highly capable?

_____

50. What knowledge have you gained from a friend or relative?

_____